Praise for *The Day John Met Paul* and Jim O'Donnell

"*The Day John Met Paul* is ⸀ ⸀rit-
ten! It's a crucial text to ur⸀ ⸀or-
dinary research, fresh appro⸀ ⸀ ⸀
The writing itself is a kind ⸀ ⸀les
bookshelf."
— Ray Coleman, autl ⸀ ⸀...uon: *The Definitive Biography*

"A spellbinding, magical tale . . . *The Day John Met Paul* reads like
a drama, a thriller even . . . It's an enchanting, poetic time-
machine of a book . . . You won't be able to put the bloody book
down." —Andy David, *Record Collector*

"The idea for this book is so obvious—and so courageous—that it
almost takes the breath away . . . Psychologically insightful, bril-
liantly researched. . . . An astonishing account. . . . Indispens-
able." —*The Beatles Monthly*

"A superb re-creation of a moment in music history based on de-
tailed research and imaginative insight. Jim O'Donnell has a reporter's curiosity, a rock 'n' roller's heart, and he writes like a
lyrical Irish poet."
—Michael Lydon, a founding editor of *Rolling Stone*

"If you think every possible book on the Beatles has been written,
Jim O'Donnell proves you wrong." —*Good Day Sunshine*

"Incredible research . . . By the time John Meets Paul, the book
just explodes!" —BBC Radio

"When it comes to writing about music, Jim O'Donnell is a favorite of mine." —Les Paul

"*The Day John Met Paul* is brilliant. I can't fault it."
—Colin Hanton, former member of The Quarry Men
(John Lennon's first band)

PENGUIN BOOKS

THE DAY JOHN MET PAUL

Jim O'Donnell, a veteran author and journalist, is the author of three rock music books: *Wonderful Tonight*, *Born to Rock*, and *The Rock Book*. He is a member of the New York Chapter of the National Academy of Recording Arts and Sciences. O'Donnell does his best thinking at the Jersey Shore, which he calls, "Springsteen country, America's Liverpool."

PENGUIN BOOKS

JIM O'DONNELL

An
Hour-by-Hour
Account
of How the
Beatles
Began

THE DAY
JOHN MET PAUL

PENGUIN BOOKS
Published by the Penguin Group
Penguin Books USA Inc., 375 Hudson Street,
New York, New York 10014, U.S.A.
Penguin Books Ltd, 27 Wrights Lane,
London W8 5TZ, England
Penguin Books Australia Ltd, Ringwood,
Victoria, Australia
Penguin Books Canada Ltd, 10 Alcorn Avenue,
Toronto, Ontario, Canada M4V 3B2
Penguin Books (N.Z.) Ltd, 182–190 Wairau Road,
Auckland 10, New Zealand

Penguin Books Ltd, Registered Offices:
Harmondsworth, Middlesex, England

First published in the United States of America by Hall of Fame Books 1994
This edition with a new afterword published in Penguin Books 1996

10 9 8 7 6 5 4 3 2 1

LIBRARY OF CONGRESS CATALOGING IN PUBLICATION DATA
O'Donnell, Jim.
     The day John met Paul: an hour-by-hour account of how the Beatles
began/Jim O'Donnell.
          p.   cm.
     Includes bibliographical references (p.).
     ISBN 0 14 02.5301 7 (pbk.)
     1. Beatles—History—Chronology.   I. Title.
ML421.B403   1996
782.42166'092'2—dc20   95–564
[B]

Printed in the United States of America
Set in Garamond #3
Designed by Jessica Shatan

Dedicated in loving memory of my mother,

VERA M. O'DONNELL (1913–1993),

forever in our hearts,

now in God's hands.

CONTENTS

AUTHOR'S NOTE

This is a true story, based on eight years of research, travel, observation, and interviews. I did not change facts, nor create dialogue.

I did, however, take some liberties with the narrative. I indulged in dramatization when describing day-to-day physical details—hand gestures, birds in flight, sleep movements, daily routines, children's horseplay, and the like. I also took it upon myself to occasionally depict what some characters thought and felt, although such ruminations were based on the facts at hand.

Otherwise, all information and events—from the hour-by-hour weather patterns to the dates on (the real) Eleanor Rigby's grave—are the hard facts of a real story.

Part I

THE MORNING HOURS

EARLY A.M.

The tousle-haired teenager in the small bedroom sleeps
the deep sleep of the young. His breathing is soft and
slow and steady. He removes a hand from under the sheets
and unconsciously rubs the upper bridge of his angular
nose at the spot where his glasses rest when he's reading.
The glasses are on his little dresser. The thick lenses in
their thick black rims eyeball him from across the bedroom above the front porch of 251 Menlove Avenue, Liverpool, England. In his golden slumbers, the tall teen can't
know that the day ahead will be the kind around which
bedtime stories are woven—a day that will spawn history,
a day of magic.

The time is 3:33 A.M. The date is Saturday, July 6,
1957. The season is summer, the time of year when magic
and music and memory become one. It is a soft-scented
morning as Liverpool reposes in black velvet. The temperature is 60 degrees, the humidity is 94 percent, and

the feeling in the opaque darkness is sultry. It is, in fact, the beginning of the tenth day of a heat wave that has fire stormed its way across Western Europe. The weather has gone crazy. The sun has been brazen. Day by day it has beaten down on Western Europe like a flaming blowtorch. Yesterday, July 5, it was 98 degrees in Italy, 99 in Vienna, 125 in Prague—not kind to old cities or to old bones. It has been not just a heat wave but an atmospheric conflagration.

Now, in this early July A.M., the day comes up molten hot again, and Western Europe will be sunbaked. The predawn humidity pours through the tenebrous lanes and fields and piers of Liverpool. It is bizarre weather for this city where an 80 degree day is considered a scorcher even in summertime. The sky wears a gunmetal flatcap. It gives Liverpool a ghostly cast. In a Liverpool suburb, a lone blackbird cocks its head and goes for a high note. The bird hits it. It finds the color of night to be in good taste. A small covey of sparrows begins to chatter. A fluttering robin, more business-school than communications-school oriented, takes the express lane between two sycamore trees and looks for worms in a flower bed.

At 3:45 A.M. the teenager in the seven-by-eleven-foot room on Menlove Avenue has moved not a whit. He lives on a wide boulevard of a street. The road is a "dual carriageway"—two lanes in each direction. A tall hedge runs down the middle, over obsolete trolley tracks. An occasional car or taxi or truck passes by and sails a little ferry of yellow across the teen's bedroom ceiling. On the ceiling is a large poster of the blonde French actress Brigitte Bardot. The passing headlights make her hair seem candlelit. There is another poster in the room. It's of Elvis Presley. In this deepest dark of night, neither the boy nor his power-prescription specs would be able to easily see the poster, even though the landing light is on in the hall.

The only bright illumination in Liverpool at this hour is the Pier Head clock a few miles away. The giant old clock gives the River Mersey an iridescent splendor. Each A.M., as the fine sands of the new day begin their run to the bottom of the glass, the clock gives the waterfront a fresh coat of yellow. Its glow caroms off the river in little glints, making beauty out of the implacable enemy, time. The clock commands a noble view of the river. It looks out from under one of the two green eighteen-foot Liver Bird statues that perch atop the Royal Liver Building.

The clock's hands point to 3:56 A.M. The sky is a dark silver. A sea breeze combs the dockside. There is a mist over the Mersey. The river makes a coruscating portrait of Liverpool's dock lights. A total of seven and a half miles of docks form the hub of the city's shipping business. Wharves and warehouses and workers keep up the charade that life is fair. The workers' faces are sullen. Memories of better days keep their souls intact. A sailor stares at a giant, unused crane and sings the spirit of his far-off home port into the clammy Liverpool night.

A few clouds scud behind the Pier Head clock on the Royal Liver Building. There is a warm feeling to the structure. Even in grimy gray, it holds a solemn sedateness. Amongst the seagulls, against the sea wind, there is the mournful piping of a ship's horn. It is a sound and scene that the slumbering teenager knows well. He often goes to the waterfront and stares longingly after ships as they shove off on their seafaring journeys.

It's 4 A.M. The sky has lightened, but Liverpool is still a dark chalk ledge under a bluish blackboard. More birds send out wake-up calls. The air is thick and still. On Menlove Avenue the teenager, John Winston Lennon, snoozes in the wee hours. He lives there with his aunt, three cats, and a dog named Sally. On this day, he is sixteen years, eight months, three weeks, and six days old, three months away from his seventeenth birthday. His fingers are callused and he has long sideburns. In a matter of days he finishes school. Today being Saturday, the classrooms are locked. Not much could please the young Lennon more.

The screenless leaded windows of his room are opened out and up. His shirt hangs on a doorknob; his pants are on his dresser next to his glasses; his socks are on the extension speaker hooked up to the parlor radio-phonograph downstairs. His peach crate of a bedroom is one of seven rooms in the semidetached brick villa. The rooms are pleasant and cozy. The home's nickname is "Mendips," after the lush green English hills. They name houses to give them a touch of individuality. Owned by the Smith family, the two-story home features bay windows and flower beds and hedges in a manicured front garden. At this hour, the buds of May flash bright July petals. A geranium blossom yawns in the sable silence.

Some breeze-stirred blades of grass reach over to attempt a polite stifle.

The middle-class home sits snugly on a borderline: it is technically in the ward of Allerton, but carries the postmark of the village of Woolton. In essence, the house is in Allerton by map, but in Woolton by shopping, public transportation, milkman, postal address, and parish. One might say 251 Menlove Avenue *sleeps* in Allerton, but *lives* in Woolton. Or, more to the point, that the home's *brain* is in Allerton, but its *mind* is in Woolton.

The village is Woolton; the house is Mendips; the county is Lancashire; the country is England. But no geographical factor has shaped the character of the sideburned teenager as much as the *city*—which is Liverpool. By 4:14 A.M. the Liverpool sky is a pale blue canopy. Smokestacks feed dark blue plumes into the shark teeth of the industrial skyline. There's some light in the sky. The slow brightening is serene.

The serenity overhead clashes with the earthly mood of Liverpool. The city has been charged of late—charged with the current of current events, and charged with change. The place is still abuzz over the visit of Queen Elizabeth on Tuesday, June 25. The queen graced the city to share in the 750th anniversary of Liverpool's charter. The theme of the yearlong charter celebrations is "Liverpool Leads." From house-decorating competitions to fancy flower displays, residents are taking the anniversary to heart and making a memorable time of it.

In terms of change, Liverpool is in the midst of major

surgery on what amounts to a city's backbone: its transportation. The year 1957 marks the beginning of two fundamental changes in how people get around the skeleton of Liverpool's streets. In December of the previous year, the city closed down the pounding steel-wheeled, sixteen-foot-high Liverpool Overhead Railway. And trams are being phased out in favor of buses and motorcars. In two months, the Baby Grand 293 will drive the last route for Liverpool trams. The pungent scent of black leather tram seats will waft into an era bygone.

For many, the loss of the overhead train and the tram car is a beheading of their city's past. In their memory, the head of the city is the mode of its transportation. Now the head is being lopped off. The older the Liverpool denizen, the greater his sense that the city is losing its identity as it loses its overhead and tram lines.

At 4:20 A.M., there are few trying to figure out the geometry of Liverpool's blue-shadowed streets. Yet already, this early, there is a liveliness to Liverpool. The city is far from the wealthiest in the world, but it daily produces a million dollars-worth of personality. At heart, Liverpool is a city lit with wit. The city sits on an undeviating sandstone slope. The word *Liverpool* derives from a Norse word meaning "pool of the slopes." Liverpool wit runs through the storybook city every day like a stream of gold.

The public image of Liverpool is a city of ships and wits; footballers and street brawlers; nasal accents and nasty accidents; liners of might and ladies of the night.

An invaluable landmass of English life, this uptempo city is 202 miles northwest of London. It holds down the right bank of the River Mersey and is the second largest port in the British Isles. In 1957, there is a polyglot population of 768,700: English, Irish, African, Chinese. Industrial plants and kingsize parks make it a city of both ash and grass; of grotesque grinding and garrulous gardens.

The grass—and everything else in Liverpool—nearly turned to ash in the early 1940s. During World War II, Hitler pounded the Liverpool landscape. Besides warehouses and plants, personal dwellings took a beating. Almost 7,000 homes were demolished and another 125,000 were left partly standing. By 1957, things are starting to settle down for the city. The people are resilient and tough. The living standard is shifting into a postwar upswing. Life is getting back to normal, if slowly.

Unfortunately, the city buildings cannot renew themselves as fast as the people can. Official relandscaping programs began five years ago, in 1952. But the task is titanic and the pace is snail-like. So by 1957, the bleeding of postwar Liverpool has stopped, but the scars are still fresh. The experience of the war still seems to exact a daily pound of flesh. The terrain is jagged with blast marks and pits and cavities of earth. There are weed patches on the bombsites. The center of the city has the texture of an old shoe that has been cobbled one too many times. The war has bled Liverpool to the point where its face has turned black as wet coal. At 4:31 A.M., black-sooted and crater-ridden, it looks like England's dark side of the moon. A filmy gray sky blankets the burnt-out shell of a car on the Dock Road.

Three miles south of Liverpool's City Centre dock area, the teenager on Menlove Avenue, in better-heeled Woolton, sleeps like a cat. From the waterfront to Woolton is a classic city-to-suburb sojourn. Of Liverpool's 27,818 acres, the suburban village of Woolton occupies 2,181, most of it winding roads and tall trees. The village is an emerald in the rusty ring of industrial Liverpool. The air is cleaner and the streets are quieter and the time moves more slowly. This lovely jewel of a village is a patchwork of parks and churches and shops and homes that never lock their doors. Woolton is genteel—a big garden of a suburb that works hard to keep a village veneer. The year may be 1957, but there are no supermarkets here. The place is that untinctured by modernity. The people lead lives that are fruitful, family-centered, and fixed to the wonders of nature. Fame is not a value here. The village has thriven in this peaceful way.

The woodsy streets are mostly unpeopled at this hour. You could stand on any corner, look up and down the lane, and wonder if this sleepy little town has taken to the horseless carriage yet. Sleep for some, however, is not as engulfing as usual. The reason is that this is the biggest day of the year in Woolton: the St. Peter's Parish Church Garden Fête, an annual fair held in early summer for the benefit of the church.

For the less-than-cosmopolitan village, it is a party, fair, parade, feast, carnival, social, dance, circus, concert, and picnic all rolled into one. The event, in one way or the other, touches every doorstep in the parish. The community focalizes on this day. Virtually everyone takes part— kids, teens, adults, elderly. Many people, actually, already slowed themselves down on Thursday and Friday, husbanding their energy for the Big Day.

The teenager on Menlove Avenue does not sleep fretfully, even though the Big Day is bigger for him than for most. He plays guitar and has a band that will be playing at the church fête. It's the first time that a teenage pop band has ever been asked to play for the occasion, although the group not only isn't the main event of the day, it isn't even the main *musical* event. The main event, the big attraction, is a dog show. As for music, the teen band has been invited as a novelty act for a bit of fun. The idea is that flavoring the show with a youngish rock'n'rollish sound will provide a loose flip side to the day's standard fare, as well as pleasing the kids.

A marvel of movement, rock'n'roll in the fifties has hit England as hard as any wartime firepower. It pervades the quotidian life of the country like an odorless gas. The American rock guitar has crossed swords with the British royal scepter, and even the windows of Woolton are rattling. Rock isn't only lasting: it daily dispatches three-chorded warships of rock'n'roll platoons over the radio.

The talismanic power of the three chords is not lost on the Woolton teenager named Lennon. He is immersed in the music. His thoughts pullulate with the beat of it. He has a guitar and it is the bright trophy of his life. The guitar has no case. It doesn't need one. He doesn't put it away. From the day Lennon got it, the guitar has spent more time airborne than Lindbergh.

It's 4:42 A.M. and a scant easterly breeze brushes the budding musician in his bed on Menlove Avenue. Down the street, around the corner of Beaconsfield Road, another breeze curls through the rococo iron grating of the gates at Strawberry Field, seven foot four inches at their highest point. The gates guard a Salvation Army orphanage that presently accommodates twenty children. They also enclose several acres of thick foliage. The summer trees wear a conceited green. Some of teenage Lennon's best hours are spent on these grounds. He loves to laugh and play and dream here.

By a quarter to five in the morning, Woolton's myriad birds are in full song. They chatter away, fly to new eaves, and issue more tunes from the tall trees. Some of the trees are so tall, they seem to flirt with the whitening sky.

Dawn awaits behind Woolton's trees and church spires.

DAWN

The ashen sky bides its time in anticipation of the first glimmer of daylight. On the peppery gutter that is the Mersey River, a tugboat pants out to sea. Packs of cats hunt out rats on the shadowy docks. A few miles up-country, in the village of Woolton, the air is clotted with humidity. An owl sends a spooky hoot into the Woolton wildwood. Summer is alive. Woolton is in bloom. A draft out of the east picks up. The teenager on 251 Menlove Avenue slumbers tranquilly in the somnolent setting.

There's a recurrent dream that the young man has. Lennon's deepest sense of reality issues from his dreams. It's not certain whether he dreams it this July A.M. If he does, his mind has him playing with his friends in the twilit emanations of Strawberry Field. There's the sudden beating of giant, thundering, ground-jolting hoofs behind him. The sound is threatening—definitely *not* Bambi making a cameo appearance on the mind screen of the teen. He turns around and sees a horse as big as a house galloping right at him. He spreads his arms, raises his eyes to a surreal sky, and flies away toward his house on Menlove Avenue.

About a mile from Menlove—the exact distance depending on whether you go around or across the pool-table green golf course—another Liverpool teenager is getting his beauty sleep. His eyelashes are long and dark and sheeny. They're perfectly still against a white pillowcase that has a fragrance of lavender. His address is 20 Forthlin Road, Allerton, a suburb less lushly wooded than Woolton. The little brick residence was built by the Corporation of Liverpool, making it a "council house." Entrenched in a row of houses pressed against each other, it purveys an unassuming ambience. The place has tidy hedges and a verdant backyard and graceful white curtains. A breath of air blows the net curtains back and forth in the teenager's room. His slumber at this presunup hour is fathomless. He's not aware that the pink dawn is ready.

The tallest point in the area is over a mile away, back in Woolton: the St. Peter's Parish Church. It is a majestic edifice of pale red sandstone. The building is cut from the local quarry, hacked out with an ocean of male Liverpool sweat. It is a towering figure of a church, its Gothic spires pointing lofty fingers at the grayish summer sky. Inside the belfry of the tower is an engraved inscription: THE WORLD IS FULL OF SHADOWS, BUT THE SUN MAKES THEM ALL.

The clock on the red sandstone church has gold hands and gold Roman numerals on a black face. As the seconds of the minutes of the hours of July 6, 1957, tick on, the golden hands reach 4:51 A.M. The temperature is 61 degrees. The birds in the trees surrounding the church sound like a pet shop at feeding time. The humidity still holds at a soupy 94 percent. As the sun comes up over the rim of the earth, the clouds are purfled with red. The St. Peter's Church spires catch the first shiny rays. Streaks of gold break up the larger clouds. The sky lightens into several longish blue lakes. A few clouds begin to bleach. The sun fingers the church. Then it bronzes the glittering clock hands.

Lovely day for a wedding . . .

The morning light brings a trace of ebullience even to the mossy cemetery next to St. Peter's Church. The churchyard is an army of superannuated gravestones standing at varying degrees of crooked attention. The timeworn inscriptions tell of Liverpool people who will never wake to a good day's sunshine. Buried near the Church Road side of the graveyard is the body of a woman named Eleanor Rigby. Her dates are August 29, 1895, to October 10, 1939. She lived at 8 Vale Road, Woolton, and she died at forty-four. Her gravestone tenders a simple inscription: ASLEEP, as if her name would one day be on the lips of the awake.

The St. Peter's bell chimes a lonesome five o'clock. The teenager behind the billowy curtains of Forthlin Road, Allerton, doesn't hear the chimes. There is the hint of a light summer breeze in the room. The teen's name is

James Paul McCartney. He lives with his father and younger brother. Born on June 18, 1942, he's eighteen days into his fifteenth year. Under his lavender-scented pillow is a pair of headphones hooked up to the radio downstairs. He often lies in bed, straight and still as a poker, listening to rock'n'roll through the headphones. Around him spins the dreary, drudging, daily world; through the rock'n'roll headphones marches a fantastic pageant.

As the sun moves higher, the boy in the bed is left to his dreams. And dreamer he is. He has as many dreams as there are cobblestones in the whole of the British Isles. Big dreams they are—the only kind teenagers have. His biggest dream is of the pageant: like the teenager on Menlove Avenue, he wants to become as good as his rock'n'roll idols. Indeed, by 1957, rock swings a lustrous lantern through the darker corridors of many a teen dream.

Since its inception in the early fifties, rock has been a contagion of colossal power. From the way teens are taking to the music, you'd think that rock'n'roll was invented so that kids would have something to do between childhood and adulthood. With its unmistakably mutinous undertones, rock provides a musical score for the twilight universe that is adolescence. It spotlights teens as a group unto themselves. To parents, it is adolescence scrambled —confusion compounded. To teens, it is a personalized declaration of independence.

A thumbnail chronology of 1950s rock dates is a thumbnail chronology of a war between young and old.

In 1954, rock rolled a bold howitzer onto bald Eisenhower's turf, as a few American rock songs shot into the record charts. In 1955, the firepower started when Bill Haley's "Rock Around the Clock" reached Number One—in both the U.S. and England—and Chuck Berry's "Maybellene" began to scream. In 1956, rock landed two direct hits: Elvis took over and Little Richard wailed.

By 1957, rock is racing like a tidal wave across the flat open ocean of the pop charts, and the establishment is not liking it any too much. As successful as the form is by this time, most adults—and the music industry itself— still look at rock condescendingly. On July 1, 1957, the music trade publication *Billboard* runs a front-page story which says: " 'Good music' may be making a comeback on the best-seller charts, but rock'n'roll discs continue to dominate the pop market." The new sound is fighting a generational, musical, social, personal war with society. Anything could happen next.

And it does.

For, while exploding society's walls, rock'n'roll is *im*-ploding in the hearts of some teenagers from an old English seaport called Liverpool.

In the Liverpool of 1957, as in the rest of England, teens *listen* to rock, *buy* rock, and *dance* to rock. But when it comes to teens *performing*, the clamor of choice is something called skiffle. Played on any number of acoustic guitars, washboards, and a tea-chest bass, skiffle is a light, loose, nasal-ridden entertainment. If it was any more nasal they'd have to call it sniffle. It is a whisking, wheezing, washy whoop. If a guitar could get asthma, skiffle is what it would sound like on a bad day. It barely moves, but it gives the kids who play it the scent of rock'n'roll on their fingers—gives them a whiff of the riff.

Before skiffle, the only British kids playing music in public were parading for the Boy Scouts Drum and Bugle Corps. Skiffle unites English teenagers as nothing ever has before. Kids standing on Liverpool corners, acoustic guitars in hand, become about as common as sailor hats. The main reason that skiffle lodges itself as England's on-the-street teen scream is that anyone can play it. Another reason is that the instruments are easy to get. The sound is natural—as homemade as a chat over the garden wall, as English as a hot cup of tea. Learn a few chords and get together with your friends. What emerges is more like a clubby amalgamation than a band. They play on piers, in coffee bars, town halls, pubs, youth clubs, social clubs, and homes.

For all its amateurity, skiffle has an old pro as its progenitor. An Englishman named Lonnie Donegan scored a Top Ten hit with "Rock Island Line" in 1956 and started Britain's first teenage media mania. He employs a western lilt and an easy beat, drawing on American folk, blues, and jazz. Some of his other tunes include "The Cumberland Gap," "Railroad Bill," and "Midnight Special." Donegan's songs give teens a simple music they can play on simple instruments. It serves as a more accessible, less frenetic, alternative to rock'n'roll.

By 1957, although skiffle is still riding high, some

teens are beginning to perceive it as a local fad, already rickety. Many believe it will give way to rock as surely as trams are giving way to buses. In the context of Elvis, skiffle seems like rock'n'roll on training wheels; a rehearsal, a scrimmage to loosen up for league play. Rock is as big and hard as Gibraltar; skiffle is a rock candy flavor of the week. A few teens even exchange their washboards for amplifiers. The argument of skiffle versus rock prevails among British youth in 1957.

Otherwise, the year opened on a harmonious note for the Liverpool music scene. On January 16, a traditional jazz club hung out a shingle at 10a Mathew Street. An old wine crypt thereupon metamorphosed into an entertainment venue called The Cavern. The place adopted its name from a Parisian spot known as Le Caveau Français Jazz Club. Of late, the club has added skiffle on Wednesday and modern jazz on Thursday to its traditional jazz lineup.

On February 6, at London's Dominion Theatre, the English had their first look at rock'n'roll's pathfinder, Bill Haley. It had been Haley's song, "Rock Around the Clock," that first broke the music to the British Empire. Swinging his way-too-big guitar, sweating hot comets down his moon-shaped face, a big curl hanging down his forehead like a tabloid-sized comma, Haley flew through thirteen tunes in thirty minutes. The crowd of three thousand adored him. Rock's original settler played Liverpool later in the month, on February 20. He meets up with a relative there, as well.

The other monarchs of the music are also on the move in '57. Chuck Berry—brandishing his guitar as if he were using it to shoot rapids—would do 240 one-nighters that year. In April, Jerry Lee Lewis cut a record called "Whole Lotta Shakin' Goin' On." In July, a Buddy Holly song called "That'll Be the Day" is earmarked as a chart-buster. Also that month, Capitol Records introduces a new recording concept called stereo.

In early July 1957, Elvis Presley asserted his rock supremacy among the young. His song "Teddy Bear" dethroned Pat Boone's "Love Letters in the Sand" from the Number One seat in the United States. At the same time, in the United Kingdom, his "All Shook Up" shook Lonnie Donegan's "Gamblin' Man/Puttin' on the Style" out of the top seat. Elvis did not get to savor his two-fisted-sockeroo, however. On July 4, he found out that twenty-four-year-old Judy Tyler had been killed in a car crash. She had starred with him in his most recent picture, *Jailhouse Rock*.

To picture English rock '57, think of the music as a Trojan War between parents and kids. Lonnie Donegan was the guy who stood outside the gates and yelled up that there was a nice horsey waiting out front. Haley *was* the horsey—a harmless enough family man in a plaid sports jacket—that adults let roll inside their walls. Elvis, the first rock'n'roll warrior, was the head honcho inside—creaking open the side panels to get out, consulting with the infantryman squad of Buddy, Berry, Jerry, and Penniman. No doubt about it: rock has dawned over young

England . . . and establishment England is trying to wake up to the fact that it isn't having a bad dream.

Dawn has also passed over the Liverpool of July 6, 1957. The young dreamer named McCartney hooks his fingers into his pillow. It's 6:03 A.M., and the curtains of his room at 20 Forthlin Road maintain a steady fluttering course in the meager breeze. The sun is a soft glow in the eastern sky. Patiently, the glow tries to unknot a few more gray clouds.

Over a mile away, in the village of Woolton, the street lamps are still on. The sidewalks are clear of people. Traffic is sparse but increasing. The deferential purr of a white milk truck glides into the ears of residents on Church Road. On each side of the small electric van it says JAMES' DAIRY. The business is owned and run by Cyril and Megan James. This morning it is Megan who drives down Church Road in her unobtrusive little vehicle. There is the clanging of pint bottles as she makes her deliveries of milk and cream and butter and eggs to front and back doorsteps.

Most people take their milk in from the doorstep around 7 A.M. By the time the St. Peter's Church clock rings that hour, Woolton is summer clad in brightening blue-gray sky and moist air and clouds of motley shades. Behind the church is the long green field where the local Liverpool people will have their big garden fête today. It will be a respite from their daily labors; a day when the big, hard, spinning world will shrink to the more manageable dimensions of a *fête champêtre*. Diamonds of dew dot the Woolton field.

A pleasant bike ride away in Allerton, dreamer-teen Paul opens his eyes briefly from a cavernous doze. He turns on his side, and the dark brown hair sweeps against the fragrant white pillow case. He falls back to sleep, never dreaming that, before the newborn sun sets, he will discover gold in Liverpool.

MORNING

It's 7:24 A.M.

A fine mist drifts across the fresh-risen sun. Some slate-gray clouds threaten rain. A thin yellow paintbrush stroke outlines one thick cloud, torn at the edge. Liverpool extinguishes its night lights. On a week day, most people would be on their way to work by now. This being a Saturday, the city runs on a different track. It's a day for shopping and golfing and, in the green-maned village of Woolton, throwing a garden party.

The morning turns pesky. The humidity is high. People can tell it's going to be another hot day. They think it's going to rain, but they still want to get on the road and on the move. The heat has gotten to be too much; they want out of the city. So even at this early hour, travel out of Liverpool City Centre is heavy. It looks like a steamy Saturday in July and people are leaving town any way they can—by foot, by car, by bus, by boat, by train.

In the heated holiday rush, the 7:15 Rochdale-to-Southport train rams into the back of a stationary train at Manchester's Victoria Station. Three people are injured seriously enough to be taken to the hospital. Another thirty-one are shaken up enough to disembark. Damage to either train is minimal.

Many of those who opt to stay home—or not to hit the road until later—flip their newspapers open across the breakfast table. The *Liverpool Daily Post* calls itself "Merseyside's Own Morning Newspaper." Its lead story of Saturday, July 6, 1957, carries this headline across the top of five columns:

COMMONWEALTH PLAN
FOR ATOM TEAMWORK

The story relates how, the night before, ten British Commonwealth Prime Ministers concluded a ten-day conference in London on world affairs. Their chief finding is that first steps need to be taken in worldwide nuclear disarmament. They are also agreed that the main goal of all Commonwealth governments is the attainment of world peace.

In 1957, Britain, the U.S., and the U.S.S.R. are the only three countries to have nuclear power. Two months earlier, in May, Britain had tested an atomic weapon on Christmas Island. Although the test had been a success,

Britain didn't have a modern plane capable of transporting the bomb. The British V-bomber forces had neither the size nor the strength of, say, the American B-52.

Another major news story in this morning's *Liverpool Daily Post* tells how the United States yesterday, on July 5, exploded an atomic bomb in Nevada. The test blast was more powerful than any atomic bomb thus far—four times stronger than the one dropped on Hiroshima. It scorched the western skies for over 500 miles and shook the earth to the point that communities 30 miles away felt the shock. A brigade of 2,000 Marines watched the big bang from trenches 5,700 yards from the center of detonation. Twenty-five miles northeast of the test site, the shock wave shattered windows and frames, punched out doors and casings, and produced bulges in metal buildings.

On June 24, 1957, within the past two weeks, three of the world's leading atomic physicists have distributed a report declaring that radioactive fallout from the newer atomic bombs would be reduced by 95 percent. The scientists—Edward Teller, Ernest Lawrence, and Mark Mills—also claimed that, with more work, there could be an atomic bomb whose radioactive fallout would be "essentially negligible." The government describes the July 5 fallout in Nevada as "minute and insignificant." In their reporting, most European newspapers stress the power of the bomb; most American papers play up the stunning visual aspects of the mushroom cloud.

The morning cloud over Liverpool is nearly complete by 8:02 A.M. The humidity is 94 percent and the temperature is already 65 degrees. By this hour, on this day, most of the townspeople of Woolton are up and about—at least the adult townspeople. Some of their homes have little wooden fences in front; others feature castle-shaped chimney pots, still others, thick brass door knockers. Many houses draw their essence from the red sandstone of the local quarry. From the outside, the homes stand becalmed. From the inside, they quiver with the fun of getting in gear for a communitywide party.

The crowning moment of the party will be a coronation. A local girl will have the honor of being crowned Woolton's 1957 Rose Queen. Other young people on display at the fête will be the Rose Queen's little royal assistants, children in costumes or fancy dress, the St. Peter's Youth Club, Girl Guides, Boy Scouts, Brownies, Discoverers, and Cubs, and a local musical act called the Quarry Men Skiffle Group. Before the fête, many of these young people will ride through Woolton on the back of a lorry —a big, long, flattop truck with no sides. The procession will include a total of five lorries—mostly coal lorries— loaned by local merchants.

Around 8:30 A.M., the merchants start driving their lorries toward St. Peter's Church on Church Road. That's where the young people will climb aboard for the start of the procession. The lorries have been hosed down and cleaned the night before. They wend their way through the morning hours of Woolton. The streets are pleasant, small and quaint and softened with age. The lorries can make their turns deftly because the street corners are rounded off, not pointed. The Woolton street names are exhibited on plaques on corner walls. They seem more like decorations than directions. The lorries crawl up Church Road like long, undulating, motorized, gray caterpillars climbing up the bark of an old tree.

The St. Peter's Church bell rings nine o'clock. The lorries are in place, parked near the church on Church Road. Over on Woolton Street, a shopkeeper puts a two-sided stand-up sidewalk ad in front of his store. His shop is called Gillard's Confectioners. The ad is for a cigarette called Players. On either side, the sidewalk ad bears this alliterative request: "Players, Please."

It's four minutes past nine when a greengrocer named Stan Gerkin draws up his horse and wagon on Manor Road for his first stop of the day. A tall, slim man of few words, he conducts his business under the name of Mr. Simcox. He stands on Woolton street corners each day, under his gray flatcap, selling fruits and vegetables. For a few special customers, he knocks on doors. Known for freshness of product and fairness of price, he makes a good living. The bag on the leather strap over his shoulder has several sections filled with coins for making change. He stays about half an hour at each corner, his horse flicking its ears to chase flies, as his customers arrive and depart. Saturday is always busy for the vendor. Around 9:30 on this vapory morn, Mr. Simcox starts for his second stop, Hunt's Cross Avenue. There is the sound of clopping hoofs.

On Church Road they've started decorating the lorries

for this afternoon's garden fête procession. Sunday School teachers and assorted friends find themselves knee-deep in paper roses and flags and balloons and bunting. As the decorations liven the lorries, the big topic of conversation is the weather.

The fact that the temperature is rising two or three degrees per hour is of secondary concern to the women this morning. The primary concern is: Will it rain on our parade? Will the biggest day of the year be a washout? Despite the morning cloud cover, the villagers are incredulous at the thought. They nearly always have a nice day for the fête. It is rarely rainy. To listen to some of the elderly on the morning of the '57 garden party, you'd think that it not only *would* not rain today but *could* not. There's more chance of seeing cut-glass chandeliers appear over that church field today than there is of seeing storm clouds.

But they give the issue a good jawing anyway. It helps make the possibility of rain seem less likely as they lovingly put the finishing touches on the Rose Queen's trellis. This five foot high, curving, interlacing structure will form an arch over the Rose Queen as she sits on a coal lorry and parades through town. Then, after the procession, the trellis will be moved to the church field and set up on the stage, the center of the day's events.

One of the people who will work that stage is having trouble shaking the sleep out of his brain. It's 10:08 A.M. and the tall, sideburned lad from Menlove Avenue sits in his bed with a pen in his right hand and a small spiral notebook propped up against his legs. The bed is young Lennon's workbench—for writing, reading, drawing, thinking, playing guitar; the room is his cocoon—although American music, of late, has made it a cacophonous Coca-Cola cocoon. As a boy, he felt a sense of restriction in this house known as Mendips. As a teenager, he feels impounded. He's a tidal wave in a seashell. Except for the tree house in the back garden and the glass-enclosed front porch directly under him, he regards this seven-by-eleven plot of room as the extent of his personal domain. The young man's particular sensibilities transfigure the cubbyhole. They make it a private world of imagination and memory and creation; a room that stops time.

By this time on a weekday, the teenager would have been in school long ago. Quarry Bank Grammar School is about a mile away on Harthill Road. The school is the British equivalent of an American high school set up for academic work, not trade. He usually leaves at 8 A.M. and bikes to school on his green Raleigh Lenton. Since it's a Saturday, he gets to sit in bed in his dreamy house of many windows—leaded windows, at that, which crayon and bend the light of the day. The colored-glass designs of the teenager's windows look like cat's eyes. The light through the windows this morning is poor.

In the duskiness of his little room, the young man stares through thick black-rimmed glasses at his notebook. His eyesight is weak but he rarely wears his glasses. He feels that they make him look timorous. He doesn't even like to wear them when he goes to the movies where it's dark. The eyes behind the glasses are autumn-leaf brown. The sockets are settings for an ancient gaze; sailor's eyes.

The sixteen-year-old has already taken his breakfast— a good English breakfast of fried eggs, sausages, and toast. He sits on his bed and tries to bore a hole in his notebook with his imagination. He's still in a shallow half-sleep. The rust-colored hair is mussed. He clears the morning phlegm from his throat and stares hard at the blank page before him. At length, he sees the hole in the paper open up and he dives in headfirst, propelling the pen. He enters his fugue. The undertow takes him. The eyes may be sub-par, but there is quality to his inner vision. He has a shoreless imagination. If his creativity had ever seeped into Mendips's wood beams, the house would have transmogrified, levitated, and flown away—the Taj Mahal in a Wizard of Oz tornado . . . Taj Mendips . . .

He writes fast—just as he thinks fast, talks fast, walks fast. It's an inventive mind at work, bright as a diamond. He has his own typewriter in the room but prefers the notebooks. He keeps a stack of notebooks, which he started doing at age seven. They contain jokes, stories, poems, jottings, drawings, cartoons, and clippings of film and sports stars. Written on the cover of one of the books is "Sport, Speed and Illustrated. Edited and Illustrated by J. W. Lennon." The notebooks are small and spiralbound. The ideas in them are large and spiral. For the young Lennon, the word *idea* is practically synonymous with the sentence, *I dream*, so the notebooks have a chimerical quality to them. The approach is witty, the tone is rebellious, and the style is unconventional.

The volume and quality of the writing disclose the volume and quality of their creator's reading. It's a habit that at times lends a pallor to the young man's face. For Christmas and his birthday, he always liked to receive books as much as toys. Some favorites are Richmal Crompton's *Just William* series about a mischievous middle-class youth; Lewis Carroll's *Alice in Wonderland* and *Through the Looking Glass*; and Robert Louis Stevenson's *Treasure Island*. In his childhood days, Lennon had enjoyed the Stevenson book; now in his teen daze, he has already figured out that the place you're standing on is your Treasure Island—whether the place is the West Indies or Woolton; whether you're Long John Silver or John Winston Lennon. So the teenager hunts for buried treasure in the sights and sounds and streets and souls and stories of Liverpool.

He finds himself treasuring self-expression. It takes the form of words, images, and, most recently, sound. Although a young man, he maintains a child's ear. He finds play in sounds—sounds of the voice, sounds of day-to-day life, sounds of the body, sounds of musical instruments, sounds of nature. He hears the infinity of sounds and plays with them incessantly. His puns are definitely intended. He hears the name of Queen Elizabeth's sister —Princess Margaret—and it becomes "Priceless Margarine." Whether he's a babbling lunatic or a budding laureate, no one's sure.

Nor is anyone sure exactly where all this creativity

comes from. His family background is as fractured as the Liverpool landscape. Lennon has been raised by his mother's sister, Mary Elizabeth Smith (maiden name, Stanley). Known to John as Aunt Mimi, she is the oldest of five sisters. His mother, Julia, is the next to youngest. For most of the boy's life, his father, Alfred, has been away at sea. In the mid-1940s, Julia had given up her son to Aunt Mimi and her husband George to raise. Julia presently lives with a fellow named John Dykins as his common-law wife.

On June 5, 1955, the boy's broken family life had suffered another smashup with the death of Uncle George, his paternal guardian. A six-foot dairyman, he had been a tender-hearted man with dove gray hair and homespun philosophies. He had helped John forget that he hadn't seen his father since 1946 by teaching the boy how to read. John's first lessons had been the headlines in a local newspaper, the *Liverpool Echo*.

By 1957, the teenage Lennon's sense of family is a female-dominated one. He can tell that the five Stanley sisters run the show—and do a pretty good job of it. The street he lives on may be Menlove, but the family runs on women-love. Of the five sisters he is, naturally, closest to two. In essence, the guy with the sailor's eyes and harpoon wit has come to realize, by age sixteen, that he has an anchor for an aunt and a mast for a mother.

Mary Elizabeth Smith has been Lennon's aunt, his mother, his guardian, his guardian angel. She has given him selfless care since the day he arrived on Menlove Avenue. She is house-proud and has found the time to stay that way. The home has been kept tidy—even when she had to take in lodgers for extra income. In dealing with her sister's son, she has been a strict taskmaster. She has determined eyes, dark hair, a firm mouth, and a granite will. Often she castigates her charge for behavior that runs afoul of her deep-seated conservatism.

The flip side of the ultraprecise aunt who brought Lennon up is his birth mother, the jaunty Julia. She is a garish, slim, blithe five-foot-two. The family calls her "Juliet." Her personality finds its best wrapping in a flesh pink dress resplendent with silver and gold stars across the long sky of the skirt—all tied together with fingernails and toenails in bright red polish. She lives at 1 Blomfield Road, on the Springwood council estate, about two miles from 251 Menlove Avenue. Over the years, she has been in and out—mostly out—of her son's life. The teen years bestir Lennon to start spending more and more of his time at Julia's house. It has gotten to the point where, if he has had a serious argument with his aunt, he spends the whole weekend at his mother's. Julia shares her son's outlook and sense of humor and she encourages him to be a freebird. She is the ship's mast in that she will help him press forward in whatever direction he turns. No matter what he says or does, she'll help him sail that way.

The teenage Lennon comes to feel close to both his mother and his aunt . . . just in different ways. He has a deep affection for both. So the good ship Lennon floats between its austere anchor and its mirthful mast. Yet there is one more navigational element to be reckoned in establishing the vessel's seaworthiness. And that's the fact that the captain flies the skull-and-crossbones flag of adolescence. Lennon's adolescence is at such a flash point that it could ignite a powder keg. He's living at top teen speed. His feelings are hair trigger. He's emotionally unmoored.

The fact of teenagedom is omnipresent at 251 Menlove Avenue by 1957. Adolescence has thrown up a glass wall between the teen and his aunt. They're physically around each other but can't be as close. They're often at loggerheads. Without being a worrywart, she has been at pains to keep the boy on a straight and narrow path. But his teenage behavior has contravened all she has tried to teach him.

Five years ago, Lennon had started at the top level of Quarry Bank Grammar School; now he's finishing at the lowest. He was fourteen when his school reports began to make his aunt concerned. Both his schoolwork and his behavior lapsed swiftly. He became a firebrand of a teenager—most blustery when bored. His tie at half-mast, he parades a scarlet temper and likes to fight with people who disagree with him. He also wields a potent tongue. It's the lip of a quipster. He could be puckish or pugnacious—rattle off a dozen jokes in a row or smart mouth a teacher. By his last year at Quarry Bank, school is a joke to him, a bad joke full of wasted time.

On that account, teachers find Lennon a tough customer. Authority figures have a way of sending his teenage blood pressure through the ceiling. When it comes to adults, he equates cooperation with approval, and he approves of very little about very few adults. Thus he tests for every weak link in the chain of their characters. Where adults are concerned, he's like the squirrels that run through so much of wooded Woolton: he can be friendly, but not often. Perhaps because he has grown up bereft of his father, and often of his mother—even though they were both alive—he finds it hard to trust authorities. Woolton may have been *in* his eyes . . . but he wasn't about to have a ton of wool pulled *over* them.

Consequently, he works hard at looking hard. The bright-as-a-diamond adolescent tries to come on hard as a diamond. He has evolved into an outwardly confident teen who is inwardly gnarled with the sensitivities of an artist. If there was ever a bull in a china shop, then Lennon is its two-legged antithesis: a china shop of talent in a bull-ish boy. On a personal level, the diamond-hard wit and the flair for causing trouble mask a delicate ego. Strip away all the bully bull, and what you have left is another adolescent longing to belong. He's less a rebellious boy than he is a caricature of rebellion—a notebook cartoon character consciously overacting all the bad-boy parts. He isn't just a young man who happens to be causing trouble. He is a clever young man deliberately causing trouble, and that makes the trouble double. It also makes him wild—and there's no Lennon-tamer in sight.

By this July 1957, it looks as if life itself will be the tamer—a job it does so well with its partner in crime, time. For this summer is a summer of decision for Lennon. While previous summers may have been good for nothing more than getting a tan, this one is for getting on. Decisions, directions—maybe permanent—hang over this summer. He's at a blue-veiled crossroads. It's time to shed adolescence and commit to something: an education, a job, a military post, *something*. In Lennon's case, he has the ability to do college work, but his grades are poor. The promising pupil has become a failing rowdy. His aunt had hoped he'd go into a profession—lawyer, dentist, account- ant, whatever. But her efforts to keep the teenager in line have been ineffective. He recently failed a series of tests that would have kept him on an academic course. Her chronic concern is that John will never amount to any- thing. The specter of a dead-end future haunts her. She takes some comfort in the fact that last month he had an interview at the Liverpool College of Art, and was accepted. But she has serious doubts that he will stick with it.

Like most teenagers, Lennon doesn't want to think a lot about the future. And he *never* wants to think about it in terms of giving in to the system and being trained. This morning, sitting up on his bed, his eyes still sleepy, he's plainly not thinking about it at all. There is only the here and now: Liverpool, 1957. He's the laconic linguist and he's far away in the notebook on his lap. He stops writing and stares. He tears the page out. He balls it up and tosses it into the dustbin and decides to walk the dog.

The sideburned teenager goes downstairs and enters the front parlor. The robin's-egg blue carpet picks up the gray light from the window. He pads across the carpet and sprawls on the long couch. The furniture is reproduction antique. He rests his head on a fringed throw pillow. His eyes set upon the light blue vase on the mantel. He doesn't notice the three-tiered bookcase whose shelves moan from the weight of minds such as Winston Churchill's, Oscar Wilde's, and F. Scott Fitzgerald's. There is no TV in the house. The boy unfastens his eyes from the vase and remembers that he planned to take the dog for a walk.

The dog is a little mutt named Sally. There are also three cats sidling around the place: Tich, Tim, and Sam. The dog becomes frisky as the teenager attaches the leash to her collar. In a flinty, ineradicable English accent, he tries to get the dog to calm down. The boy's mouth is thin, and when he talks, it opens very little. His hair is still bed-disheveled. He walks out into the dank morning. The air feels good. A small finger of wind strums a small smile out of his warm face. While walking the dog, he stops at the fishmonger's shop and buys hake for the cats. He returns home, takes the fish into the kitchen, and goes back up to his room. His aunt Mimi is in the morning room, rummaging through a big tin for a button. She's glad it's Saturday. If it were a school day and John was causing problems, Quarry Bank would be calling about now.

Across Woolton the ten o'clock hour is too hot for walking. But it's still the day to go to market. The lanes are congested with shoppers. The center of Woolton is a popular shopping area in Liverpool. Women, their arms full of bags, brave the morning's 70-degree heat to visit the little shops. There are a few men along, mostly to carry the groceries.

The biggest greengrocer is Brooks Grocers on Allerton

Road. The butcher at Gamble's Meats advertises in the day's newspaper: "Meat kept in Perfect Condition by Modern Refrigeration." Hence, even in his round straw hat and white apron, the butcher sweats less than most today. Clooks Bakers exhales sweet breaths that make it a tough test to pass by the shop window without stopping. Woodward Sweetshop, a candy store, runs a special on its chewy Palm Toffee, but still sells a surfeit of gob stoppers, bubble gum, and penny licorice.

Prices in general are on the high side for most people. The expense of a Liverpool life is a postwar challenge. A pound of butter costs 2 shillings, 5 pence (34¢ in 1957 American currency). At McDonnell's, a "Gents and Boys' Outfitter and Tailor" on Allerton Road, a nylon shirt goes for 46 shillings, 11 pence ($6.57). At Bensons, on St. Mary's Road, an "Ever-ready Radio, portable" is advertised at 13 pounds, 2 shillings, 6 pence ($36.75). Pram canopies for baby carriages sell for 39 shillings, 6 pence ($5.53).

At Woolton Motors on Menlove Avenue, a '52 Austin A40 van is on the lot for 235 pounds ($658). A '55 Ford Popular, "with low mileage, many extras," is going for 325 pounds ($910). Like many another motor establishment, Woolton Motors is having a busy Saturday morning. A skilled car mechanic makes 300 pounds a year ($840) and works a forty-four-hour week. It may be Saturday, but it's still a work day for him: that extra four hours. From the welder to the warehouseman to the watch repairer, many people work five and a half days a week. At 10:10 A.M., several such workers are at this moment carving their way through the local sandstone quarry.

For those not working . . . or shopping . . . or helping out with the St. Peter's Church fête . . . it's a run-of-the-mill Saturday morning. The Liverpool streets pulse with the beat of children at play. Their games run the gamut from rounders to ollies to football. Among Woolton playgrounds are the fourteen acres of Reynolds Park and the sixty-two acres of Woolton Woods. The grownups find their playgrounds on the golf courses and, for the less exercise-minded, in the sports section of the morning paper, which offers everything from snooker to water polo to cricket. The top three cricket teams in the standings are Surrey, Warwick, and Derbyshire. These July 6 standings are checked and studied with care.

An ocean away today, in Rochester, New York, a lawyer files suit in the State Supreme Court to be in the delivery room when his wife gives birth to their child. Highland Hospital, in upstate New York, has prohibited him from being there. In New Haven, Connecticut, it's announced that Yale University Press will publish a Eugene O'Neill play, *A Touch of the Poet*. The manuscript, made public by the author's widow, is the only O'Neill play that has never been published or performed.

In Tokyo, about six thousand miles from Britain, fire claims two lives and consumes a one-hundred-forty-foot-high Buddhist pagoda in Ueno Park. It's believed that the couple who are found in the charred debris had set the fire as part of a suicide pact.

In Liverpool, England, at twenty-five after ten in the morning, there's a weak wet wind out of the east. The wet wind becomes a drizzle, and by 10:36 the drizzle has become a shower. The rain kisses the parched city. Along Liverpool lanes, umbrellas sprout up like dark mushrooms. The weather rankles the workers of the St. Peter's Church garden party. Crispy new dresses become soggy. Smiles become wrinkles.

The raindrops dimple the River Mersey. A rag picker in a waterfront alley gets doused. Women in backyards pull in the morning wash. A dozen or so people scurry into the shelter of the roundabout at Penny Lane. The rain pelts the awning of the Penny Lane Cake Shop where, this Saturday, custard tarts are the hot item. Raindrops cascade down the front window of the Penny Lane Barbershop, where the tab for a short-back-and-sides cut is 1 shilling, 6 pence (21¢). Mr. Leong, a Chinese laundryman on Penny Lane, stands in the doorway of his business and watches the rain beat down on the street. He folds his arms and hopes that the crystal curtains of cloudburst don't cut down on his clientele today.

The storm outside parallels a brewing storm inside the Mimi Smith-John Lennon household. A sort of teenage tension honeycombs the house. Lennon is in the bathroom upstairs combing his hair. He has been combing it for the past twenty minutes. He rakes his hair back again and again and again. The hair is a darkish sandy color. It's long for the close-cropped, Army-topped fashion of late-fifties England. The teenager stares into the bathroom looking glass and drags the comb through his hair. He takes his eyes off his hair for a second and notices the comb. He remembers buying it in Woolworth in Penny Lane. He also remembers that the girl who sold it to him had Caribbean blue eyes. Then he stares at his own eyes and stops combing. His mind sinks into thought—goes from comb to catacomb. There's no movement for a few seconds. Then he starts combing again.

The sixteen-year-old is taking extra care this morning because of his scheduled rock'n'roll show this afternoon. He uses grease to comb the sides back and the front forward. The hair over his forehead is a tousled flag of rebellion. He has already gone through gymnast moves a little while ago to angle his ankles through somewhat tight black slacks. They're his perfunctory attempt at what are called "drainies," for drainpipes. He has also donned a checkered white and blue lumberjack shirt.

The young Lennon affects the greased hair, the not-quite-drainie trousers, and the long sideburns because of his emotional identification with what are called Teddy Boys. They slice their way through postwar British life in city street gangs. It's a teen underground movement. The name is taken from their Edwardian-style clothes. This morning is the first time that Lennon has tried to look like them. He gives himself one last glance in the looking glass. He towels off the back of his neck. It's time to leave home.

The Teddy Boy–looking teen comes downstairs. It's 10:52 A.M. His aunt is sitting at her desk with the pigeonholes. She takes one look at him and her anger flashes like red lightning. For explosive potential in this house, the teenager's appearance is a bottle of nitroglycerin. So it's no surprise that an argument commences over the all-too-familiar subject of his appearance. Aunt Mimi shudders and tells him she's repulsed by his dressing up like what amounts to nothing more than teenage hooligans. Her infuriated voice carries throughout the house.

The young man can usually find ways of getting out of these confrontations. But today he's about to play rock'n'roll for the whole big wide world of Woolton. That being the case, his teen impulse to say and do what he wants is notched up exponentially. Today he all but *smells* of rebellion. If he were a sail maker, he'd smell of tar. But today he's a rocker, and he smells of rebellion. He frowns at his aunt and becomes nettled and says he's old enough to dress as he pleases and why doesn't she give him some breathing room, anyway. His anger is white hot. Yet the words are disarmingly coaxing. Even under stress, it is a voice that moves coolly—a lynx of a larynx. His aunt gathers her eyebrows and her wits, and an argument proceeds that shakes the gold-and-blue china on the plate rack in the dining room.

It's hard to estimate how well Lennon's aunt-mother understands why there's a whole-lotta-shakin'. The fact is that adolescence—adolescence and its newborn little brother, rock'n'roll—are supplanting her. Time and music are pulling the youngster away from her. At his birth mother's house on Blomfield Road, there's a windup gramophone and extension speakers in several rooms. It's a rock'n'roll home. His mother, Julia, loves rock so much that she has a cat named Elvis.

One day in 1956, his mother played an Elvis Presley record for him on the gramophone. The music made him feel as if he had never gotten out of bed before. It was a new start. It was emancipation. He heard not so much a singer on the gramophone as a disembodied voice gliding through the air on a magic carpet woven of teenage secrets. It made him take flight as the music of the dwarves makes Tolkien's Bilbo Baggins suddenly want to trade in his walking stick for a sword. Lennon had of course heard rock'n'roll before, but it was rock'n'roll by Elvis that took him over.

To the teenager, the most important thing about the loud music is the silent feelings it gives him—feelings of intensity and fun and looseness and guiltlessness. This rock'n'roll seems to wipe the slate clean—to erase the idea that life is bound by class and money and school. The music sends a message to the young man. It tells him that there's a whole country—maybe a whole generation—that feels about life as he does: that being young could, would, *should* be fun; that success might, may, *must* be won; that repression possibly, probably, *positively* must be fought. Young John Winston Lennon isn't sure about much in his life, but of this he is sure:

Rock'n'roll is the truest thing he has ever known.

The sound calls to his deepest self. And that self answers the call. To most kids, the music is a wow; to Lennon, it is a vow—something to believe in, commit to, live out. He hears a feeling—a world—in rock music, and he is determined to step into it and live it. He has seen his childhood and his childhood dreams disappear. Now, as his adolescence nears its end, rock'n'roll is his last dream of youth. He clings to the dream. He's not ready, just yet, to take his place in the rear row of obscurity. The whole point of his life is reduced to this: be a rocker, or be a docker. And he's ready to run hard and fast and scorch his lungs to make it. At the very least, the music will help him to take wing and circle the nest; at the most, it will let him live his dreams.

In his boyhood, Lennon had fleeting experiences with the accordion and harmonica. Then he got an acoustic guitar in 1956. The first time he looked at himself in the looking glass with the guitar, the image he saw made him feel complete. He feels at home with the instrument. His very flesh feels fresh. Creativity had been his hometown; now rock'n'roll has become his university. He begins to whittle a lifestyle out of the guitar. Whenever rock'n'roll turns up on the gramophone or radio or in movies, he jumps into the songs like a pearl diver. The young Lennon dives into the music of Elvis and Little Richard and Carl Perkins, searching for pearls of teen truth. The guitar becomes the spiritual axis of his adolescent world. The teen treasures his moments with the music as a newlywed cherishes moments with a spouse. He's indefatigable in learning the instrument, practicing at all hours.

He cannot, however, practice in all places. His aunt Mimi, whose tastes run to orchestra and classical music, cannot handle "that noise." Even more, she cannot handle what she regards as John's wasting massive amounts of time at a critical point in his life. She entreats the teenager to stop playing blindman's buff with his future. To the aunt, rock'n'roll is a tornado, wreaking havoc; to Lennon, it is a tornado-*cellar*, giving shelter from a weird world ready to crash down on him. When "that noise" gets to her, or when she becomes appalled by the amount of time he's wasting practicing in his room, she banishes him out of earshot. He practices in the glass-wrapped front porch.

Conversely, and not surprisingly, the guitar gathers only good graces at his mother's home. Julia teaches him how to play the thing—or at least, to play most of it. She knows how to play the banjo, not the guitar, so she teaches him as if it's a banjo, using only the top four strings. The bottom two strings get the day off. Using her mother-of-pearl banjo and wearing a housedress of navy blue with white polka dots, she teaches her son his first song: Fats Domino's "Ain't That a Shame."

From that start, the sixteen-year-old is ready to roll, picking up songs from the radio and, especially, from records. He pays 6 shillings (84¢) for Lonnie Donegan's skiffle hit "Rock Island Line." His long fingers curled around the guitar neck, he plays and replays the record on his mother's wind-up gramophone, sifting for golden nuggets of sound. But what the fledgling guitarist has managed to steal off records or radio by July 1957 wouldn't add up to petty theft. He doesn't even know how to tune. He couldn't tune the guitar if you offered him Brigitte Bardot's home phone number for doing it. He makes several circumnavigations of the act: he lets others tune it; he tunes it like a banjo; he doesn't bother to tune at all. In terms of playing, he knows only two chords. He's still learning the basics. Yet he tries to improvise already. He's like a kid who's having so much fun with his new toy that he tosses out the instruction manual. It's an idiomorphic talent begging for structure.

While the young Lennon is unversed in the technical sense, his adolescent senses are exquisite. In Elvis, the Liverpool teenager senses the blueprint of his life. He knows he wants to *become* Elvis. What he doesn't know is that he wants to become Elvis in order to become himself. He will find himself through the Elvis ego. He obviously couldn't *be* Elvis anymore than he could be *with* his other poster idol, Brigitte Bardot. So, just as he took to the homegrown English girls around him, he takes to skiffle, the homegrown English music around him.

In March 1957, he forms a band. It's called the Black Jacks for one week and then rechristened the Quarry Men Skiffle Group. The band starts out playing predominantly the skiffle songs of Lonnie Donegan. It's actually less a band than a gathering of happy, healthy, free-floating schoolboys looking forward to summer vacation. From its founding in March, Lennon has masterminded the skiffle group, turning it gradually toward rock'n'roll. Printed at the top of the Quarry Men business card is this self-depiction: "Country • Western • Rock'n'Roll • Skiffle." But the bandleader's ambition is rock ruled. The group plays anywhere it can—parties, dances, competitions. It comes by today's St. Peter's Church fête engagement through the mother of Pete Shotton. He's one of the Quarry Men and Lennon's fair-haired best friend.

Certainly, the bandleader's aunt would never procure such a date. The public performance side of the young man's life is a furtive business in the Menlove household. That is to say, his aunt doesn't even know he has a band. Like most adolescents, he has neatly cut off his home life from his outside life. His aunt Mimi has become privy to less and less of his life outside the house. The band is something that the teenager chooses to do surreptitiously. The only problem is that today he's playing at Woolton's most public event.

At ten past eleven, the Woolton weather starts to clear. It's just misting. The sun knife-edges between cloud crevasses. A sharp shaft of morning light fills several rooms of 251 Menlove Avenue. But emotional thundersqualls are still bouncing off the walls of the house.

It's 11:31 when the tart teen cuts his cross aunt off with a good-bye wave of his hand and says he's going out. His breathing is deep and fast. Yet he still feels slept in. He asks his aunt if she's going to the St. Peter's fête today. She says she is.

He nods and walks through the front hallway toward the door. He has his guitar in his hand. He's unmindful of the wooden grandfather clock in the hallway. The clockface says 11:32 and has been plangently ticking away the seconds of his life since the moment he was born. It was with this family heirloom that Lennon was introduced to the concept of time . . . back when he had time . . . back before he became a teenager . . .

The sixteen-year-old steps out the door with a leaning stride. He squints into the glare of the brandywine sky. There is a smell of wet grass. A street puddle mirrors a bestrewn image of the sky. Lennon looks at the image. The glare makes the puddle seem opalescent. He looks up at his house. The windows of his room are flecked with raindrops. The daylight sends a kaleidoscopic array of colors through the prismatical leaded glass. He wonders how the colors look from the inside.

He stands in front of his house. The sight of the forenoon sun lifts the teenager's spirits. It reminds him that he's going to bring live rock'n'roll to Woolton Village today. His temper has gone up in flames, and he considers using alcohol to put them out. He figures he should be able to get something at an off-license, a store for carryout alcoholic beverages. He decides to stop at an off-license and study a few bottles of light ale. He wants to loosen himself up for the show this afternoon. He wants a cigarette, fishes in his pockets, but doesn't have one.

The tousle-haired teenager thinks about the show. Music suddenly fills his mind and body. He looks up and down Menlove Avenue. He knows that, when it comes to playing rock'n'roll, he's the toughest kid on the block. What he doesn't know is that he's about to meet his match.

Lennon leaves for his appointment with fate.

Part II

THE AFTERNOON HOURS

NOON

The noonday sun is a white gold. It butters Liverpool's rain-slicked cobblestones. The late-morning cloudburst has taken the edge off the humidity. But the temperature keeps climbing. It registers 76 degrees by noontime—up eleven degrees in the past four hours. With the day's roller-coaster weather taking a brightening turn for the better—and the thermometer catching fire—the morning rush to leave town becomes a noon exodus. Families pack themselves off to the cooler climes of shore and country. They head for the hills like people escaping a plague. They want out before Liverpool turns into a hot skillet again.

At midday, the Liverpool Automobile Association reports a five-mile backup at the Queensferry Bridge. Cars on the road are moving at the rate of two thousand per hour. The noon pace on the Liverpool to Prescot road is one thousand per hour. Traffic through the Mersey Tunnel is dense but proceeding. An Automobile Association spokesman issues this advisory for the day: "In their own interests, we urge motorists to use alternative routes wherever practicable in an effort to reduce congestion on the main traffic arteries."

For day-trippers without cars, it's a noontime of long lines waiting for trains and buses and ferries. The ferries have names like *Royal Iris* and *Mountwood*. Thousands take the ferry 'cross the Mersey. The river is sun spangled. A rugged young deckhand on a ferry bound for New Brighton enjoys the fresh river breezes. His grin is tight, lipless. Dozens on the boat are headed for the New Brighton Bathing Pool. The pool does a prosperous business today. Several seagulls flank the ferry. A few seem pinned to the deep summer sky as they keep perfect pace with the boat. Others swoop and swerve and skim for overboard scraps in the ferry's wake.

British Railways has three trains going to the Haydock Park Races. The trains chuff out of Liverpool Central at 12:15, 12:20, and 12:33. All three of the main railway stations clatter with itchy-footed trekkers. The Liverpool to Southport line is especially hectic. At the Pier Head, hundreds more shuffle off on buses for outlying districts of the city. Up and down Liverpool streets, double-decker buses bounce beams of sunlight off condensation-fogged windows. Many on the holiday exodus have packed picnic hampers. One popular picnic spot is Woolton Village.

It's ten past noon. The sun doesn't linger. It slips behind some clouds and pauses. The sporadic clouds contrast with Woolton's honey-golden mood today. Preparations for the

St. Peter's Church Garden Fête press toward joyful last-minute confusion. The procession through town is slated to start at 2 P.M. The St. Peter's fête is one of several garden parties in Woolton from mid-June through early July. Since the church is the center of the community, the fête is scheduled each year for the Saturday nearest June 29, the feast of St. Peter.

The event is run for the church and by the church. The purpose of the day is to bring the community together while helping St. Peter's financially. A small independent committee began organizing months before. It's like preparing for a wedding. Actual arrangements for the fête get underway in January with the booking of entertainment and the ordering of tents for the fairgrounds. In March, local students began rehearsals for lining up and marching and the like. About the same time, parents started getting dresses and costumes ready.

The big fête of the big-treed village is run this year by a Forrest—a fellow named Harry Forrest. He's a congenial electrician who can keep the work current flowing through a variety of people. Last night he supervised a flurry of activity on the field behind St. Peter's Church. Stakes were jammed into the ground so that the field could be roped off into sections; the stage was situated for the Rose Queen's crowning and musical entertainment; and the grass was groomed. Women in longish cotton dresses made pots of tea in the church hall across the street and brought cup after cup over to the men at the darkened field.

By 12:30 P.M., a carnival mood rides the noonday air.

The village's emotional thermostat is rising with the weather's. Dozens of people on the church field wear faces creased with all styles of smiles. It's more like a big family gathering than a fair. The Woolton community becomes a unit on this day each year. Close neighbors become even closer. Although there is precious little time to go—with the procession on tap at 2 P.M.—people move at a leisurely pace.

When not keeping an eye on the iffy weather, some people wonder out loud whether the field will be dry enough by the time the fête starts. The fête is held on high ground on sandstone. There are only between three and six inches of topsoil and the rock is close to the surface, so rainwater tends to drain away quickly. The field itself is on a long cascading slope behind the churchyard behind the church. From Church Road, you walk through a tree-shadowed dirt footpath next to the church. You come out near the lower part of the field. That's where the day's stage has been positioned. Over halfway up the lower field, the long wide grass clearing begins a little incline.

The smaller upper field is handsomely turned out by now with two tents near the Boy Scouts' hut. The hut is a long one-story timber building. One of the tents, in the front part of the upper field, is for first aid. It's small and green and a nurse will sit by the entrance all afternoon. The other tent is in the upper right of the field behind the scouts' hut. It's big and white and serves refreshments. At a quarter to one, several cheerful faces smile across beamed wooden tables in the white tent. Midshinhemlined women are buttering rolls and making sandwiches and unwrapping hundreds of homemade cakes. The luxuriant scent of all that pastry makes the field seem like a gargantuan outdoor bakery. The smell of fresh bakery goods and freshly cut grass is sweet in the thick July air. Anyone who just follows his nose this Saturday afternoon in Liverpool finds an excellent escape from the local frying pan.

For his particular escape, the dreaming teen of 20 Forthlin Road, Allerton, has the Woolton fête in mind. But at the moment, young James Paul McCartney is in a puttering-around-the-house mood. He has long since lifted his head from the pillow aromatized with lavender. The net curtains in his room now flutter with his cognizance. He's well scrubbed, and the bacon and eggs are finished, and his father has put away the pans. The teen's dark brown hair has a seal-skin sheen as he gets a glass of milk from the Prestcold under-the-counter refrigerator. He takes the glass into the front parlor. The room has a tiled hearth and black-and-white TV and wallpaper of three different designs: striped, oriental, and brick. There are oriental scatter rugs on the floor, off-cuts of carpet. McCartney sits down and looks over the morning paper with dark, half-sleepy eyes.

On this 1957 summer's day, McCartney's disposition is sunny. His age is fifteen years, two weeks, four days. He just turned fifteen in mid-June. He lives with his father and brother in the six-room house on a wide street with a thick privet hedge in front and a healthy apple tree in the back garden. The family has one foot barely out of working class—the other not quite into middle class. The house may be council provided, but it is suffused with middle-class ambitions.

The teenager's mother, Mary McCartney (maiden name, Mohin), had been the one in the family most intent on climbing the English social ladder. A tender but not fragile woman, she had devoted herself to her family and her work, advancing from nurse to health visitor to community midwife. Each morning, she had gone to work on her small bicycle with a wicker basket. Between her income and her husband's, the family was able to improve its mailing address several times. In the summer of '56, they moved into 20 Forthlin Road, Allerton. The front door didn't open onto a moat filled with alligators, but it was still a big step upward. The mother fed the occupants of the two-floor home with sugared apple sandwiches and Sunday roasts.

Only months after moving to Forthlin Road, on October 31, 1956, Mary McCartney died of cancer. She had been so devoutly religious that one day, in the pain of the cancer, she had reached with one hand for a crucifix and with the other for a photograph of a priest.

The death leaves her husband, Jim, to care for two boys in a cloudy financial climate. The father is only making 8 pounds ($22.40) a week in the postwar-deflated Liverpool Cotton Exchange. But he is a man of working-class background and fourteen-karat pride. He keeps the little family together and happy. His most valued possession is his wife's wedding ring; his greatest love is taking care of his boys. With his seasoned eyes and statesmanlike visage, Jim McCartney seems to epitomize the family man. He's steadfast in the role. There would be more chance of seeing a spot on his gleaming black shoes than of seeing him neglect his kids. He's often funny, sometimes firm, always loving.

Despite his financial straits, he buys his younger son, Mike, a set of drums. By 1957, Mike is a spry thirteen-year-old with a resolute aspect to his lower jaw. He's eighteen months younger than his brother Paul. Whether riding their bikes together all over Liverpool or fighting like brothers in the house, the two boys have a bond that cannot be broken.

Fifteen-year-old Paul lifts his large chocolate-brown eyes from the newspaper and decides to have a bacon butty sandwich. He has a bright, open face and a strong, pleasant voice. He's good-looking—and good-natured. His presence gives the feeling of a teenager overflowing with energy; a young man in a hurry. He likes things to be in their places—in exact little squares, if possible, like the little rectangles on the thumbtacked shelf paper in the kitchen. Most saliently, the young man is personable. His public-relations instincts are already fine-tuned by age fifteen. It comes naturally to him to be ambassadorial. He doesn't do it to win anybody's favor.

In recent years, however, he has not always been the dimpled diplomat. What changed him is the coming to town of that consistently confounding circus known as adolescence. Thus, along with the politeness plus from one side of his mouth, there is acerbic wit from the other. He takes to arguing with his father over clothes and hair. The teen wants to wear the hair high (like Tony Curtis) and the pants tight (like drainpipes).

At school, he is a young man flush with promise. He has a vigorous mind. He's quite bright. He attends the Liverpool Institute on Mount Street and stays in the top half of his class. But by this summer of '57, he feels bored and directionless. In effect, the teenage Paul McCartney is a skittish colt looking for the next high fence. Everyone expects him to pursue an academic career; he's not so sure. He has given his teachers the impression that he's going to Teachers Training College. But he truly doesn't know which loose nail to hang the hat of his future on. About the only thing in his future that he's certain of is that he's going to summer camp in a few weeks. From July 29 to August 7, he and his brother will refresh themselves in Derbyshire with the 19th City School Scouts. Other than that, the young man doesn't have a clue where he's going next. Like this 1957 summer Saturday itself, he doesn't seem to be progressing in any single direction.

The clock on Liverpool's Town Hall on High Street, off Castle Street, reads 1 P.M. The clock face hangs high up in front of the town hall's big white egg of a dome. Inside the dome is the inscription DEUS NOBIS HAEC OTIA FECIT (God Gave Us This Leisure). Atop the dome, the Roman goddess of wisdom, Minerva, sits with her spear and helmet and shield. She does not smile—possibly because of the weather. The sun is pressing the city down like an oval iron. The one o'clock temperature is 77 degrees. The

Town Hall dome looks like a discrepant giant snowcap under the broiling sun.

The afternoon heat doesn't just arrive in Liverpool. It insinuates itself into the city's daily routine. Near Town Hall, a bin man, or garbage collector, on a break takes a long swig out of a greenish, thick-glassed Coca-Cola bottle. Tavern keepers keep on their toes as hundreds of foamy pints of Guinness disappear under hundreds of gray flatcaps. A green double-decker bus sighs to a stop in front of Lewis's Department Store on Ranelagh Street. The bus is crowded with afternoon shoppers. Children make a day of riding on the upper deck. Women wheel their prams; men tip their hats. Teens transport themselves to cooler worlds via record store listening booths.

Some stores do a brisk business this Saturday and some do not. Three that do are Bonsall's Fish and Chips, Hessy's Music Store, and Smith's Fishmonger. Three that don't are the Davis Travel Agency, the cosmetics counter at Woolworth in Penny Lane, and Grassi and Rossi marble masons. The tennis courts at Reynolds Park are never idle throughout the afternoon. A couple mixes a flirtation with lunch at Calderstones Park. The public swimming bath on Allerton Road makes a big splash with Liverpool locals.

Outside of Liverpool this afternoon, in London, an American scientist is given an honorary doctorate from Birmingham University. Dr. Harold C. Urey, a Nobel Prize–winner in chemistry, tells a luncheon audience that, in the future, colleges should not emphasize science to the point of undervaluing other subjects. He recommends that universities develop curriculums which stress all aspects

of Western civilization—not just the scientific aspect. Dr.
Urey is a professor of chemistry at the Institute of Nuclear
Studies in Chicago.

In Dr. Urey's home country, the future does not seem like
something to worry about in 1957. America's future seems
as glintingly bright as the dome of its president's head.
In '57 America, a teenage girl going steady wears her
boyfriend's high school ring on a gold chain around her
neck. In the U.S.A. grownup world, 1957 is the year that
the Ford Motor Company introduces a four-wheeled imi-
tation rocket ship called the Edsel. It's a medium-priced
car in four series and eighteen models.

By this July 6, America is in its third day of the long
July Fourth Independence Day weekend. Yesterday, on
Friday, the United States Senate met for precisely twelve
seconds before the recess gavel fell. But for all intents and
purposes, the holiday really got rolling on Wednesday the
third, around 4 P.M. That's when flag-waving, fireworked-
up America took to the steering wheel. It's an annual rip
tide of people going on summer vacation together. The
National Safety Council has predicted that, because of a
projected forty-five million cars being used during the
holiday, there will be a new high in highway deaths. The
estimate is that 535 people will die in traffic accidents by
midnight Sunday. The record is 491 in 1950.

Today, Saturday, people are in the deepest depths of
their vacation relaxation. Forty-four flights are canceled at
LaGuardia Airport, New York, because there aren't

enough passengers. Twenty-one of the flights were out-
bound; twenty-three inbound. In the New York metro-
politan area, an estimated one-and-a-half million people
hit the beaches to take advantage of fair, breezy, sunny
weather. (The beaches in that estimate include Coney Island, the Rockaway beaches, Palisades Amusement Park,
and Jones Beach.) At 1:20 P.M., the ocean temperature at
Coney Island is 66 degrees. Ten minutes later, the *Bri-
tannic* arrives at New York's West 52nd Street Pier with
749 passengers from Liverpool.

Dwight D. Eisenhower, president of the United States,
spends the Saturday holiday on a golf course in Gettysburg. He plays through the afternoon at the Gettysburg
Country Club. Afterwards, he tells reporters that the day
gave him "the best nine holes I've ever had here." In major
league baseball, the American pastime, there are eight
teams in each of two leagues. St. Louis is leading the
National League by a half-game over Cincinnati. The Yan-
kees have a three-game lead over Chicago in the American
League. Yankee outfielder Mickey Mantle slugged his
thousandth career hit yesterday. He's leading the majors
with a .377 batting average.

The U.S. Department of Commerce issues a report this
afternoon indicating that, in the past year, Americans
spent more money on travel abroad than on any single
imported item. The two biggest imports are coffee and
petroleum. In American music news—academic music
news, that is—Harvard University picks today to an-
nounce the promotions of two faculty members. Dr. David

G. Hughes and Robert W. Moevs are named Assistant Professors of Music at the school.

Half of the day's real news in music—although no one will know it for a spell—is a long way off in a backyard in England. Fifteen-year-old Paul McCartney sits in a striped-folding-chair world of his own this afternoon, as he strums an orange-red cello guitar. His exterior world is a little backyard, or back garden, bound by hedges and a wooden stick fence; it's the kind of yard you could fall asleep in with a book over your face. His interior world is the sound of the guitar. At this moment, he works on the guitar with the same fervor he would work on a Boy Scout merit badge later in the summer. He can't be bothered with anybody while he's practicing. When he's concentrating on his playing, he wouldn't answer the front door if Queen Elizabeth were knocking on it.

A pot of tea simmers on the Ritemp stove in the Mc-Cartney kitchen. Despite the heat of the day, the young man always seems to stay at the "right temp" when he's playing the guitar. He's not easily encroached upon. With the guitar in hand, the temperature of his teen temperament holds steady at about a cool 50 degrees. He feels at home playing the guitar here in the back garden—a not surprising development, given that his home is a veritable garden of music. An upright piano germinates in the small front parlor. A bouquet of stringed instruments springs out of various chairs and couches. Earphones ripen like dark, curling cornstalks on the teenager's bed. Ten-inch recordings mushroom near the bottom of the well-tilled gramophone.

Postally, 20 Forthlin Road is a house in Liverpool 18. Musically, 20 Forthlin Road is a garden in its own time and place. It all depends on what music the head gardener, Jim McCartney, elects to grow. He had once been a bandleader with his own semipro musical group called Jim Mac's Jazz Band. He had even written an original instrumental work. Although at present he heads a family, not a band, he often moseys over to the piano and takes a seat. Framing the front-parlor piano is a wallpaper scene of orientals and a two-story pagoda. Like the pagoda's upward-turned roofs, the mood in the McCartney household turns upward at the upright piano. The elder McCartney strokes the keyboards and demothballs anything from a soft ballad to a stage number. He can do anything with the piano except make dinner with it. He plays cross-handed, one hand over the other until his two sons are smiling through keyboards of teeth. The moments of the family sing-alongs are rich with hilarity and affection. The boys love the man; they love the music when he plays, making for twice the joy. Sometimes the boys would even perform as a duo, calling themselves the Nurk Twins. To be sure, the McCartney house is a masterpiece of musical merriment.

So teenager Paul does not get his musical inclinations off the street. They grow from the euphonic garden of his home. What he does get on his own is a taste for the street music that is rock'n'roll. Three years ago, at age twelve, he had taken in his first concert. He had seen a British group called the Eric Delaney Band play the Liverpool Empire. Ever since, popular music had brought a warm glow to his life. But the sound didn't spellbind him. It was not until late 1956 that rock'n'roll began to infuse him to the point where he wanted to play it. The turnaround event was his mother's sudden death in October of that year.

Life for the McCartney clan had not exactly been a fast, fun wink up to that Halloween Thursday in 1956. But, to the two boys, it often seemed so. In the past few months, especially, they had been cultivating splendid new memories at their best house yet, 20 Forthlin Road, Allerton. Then their mother, Mary, found out she had breast cancer and was dead inside a month's time. Paul was fourteen; Mike was twelve. The tragedy to the two boys and their father was immense, shocking, fraught with unreality. Rosary beads were wrapped around Mary McCartney's wrists. When the coffin lid was lowered on the dedicated forty-seven-year-old woman, the heart of 20 Forthlin Road stopped. The fine new home now contains the family's biggest sorrow: it is the house that they must live in without a mother. The Singer sewing machine no longer sings. The machine's steel foot pedal feels no foot. The two boys come home from school each day and miss their mother.

The death takes its toll on both boys. Sometimes the tears last well into the night, robbing them of sleep and turning their pillows into fiery little lakes. Unlike his sons, Jim McCartney cannot go swimming in tears. He has to hold his grief in abeyance and steel himself to being both mother and father on just one income. He camouflages his daily heartache with a stoic face and much work. Along with his full-time job on the Liverpool Cotton Exchange, he rolls up his sleeves and enlists in the full-time service of dishtowels and pans and irons and grocers and butchers. There is no washing machine in the house, so he learns how to wash clothes with a bucket and a mangle in the kitchen sink.

Family and neighbors pitch in to help out. Two of Jim McCartney's sisters—known to the McCartney boys as Aunt Millie and Auntie Gin—assist in every way they can. On alternate Mondays, one of them comes over and cooks a roast and cleans and irons. On other days, they help keep the tea brewing and the fireplace lit and, as much as possible, the talk flowing. Fundamentally, they and their husbands help to keep the house a home. They help the grief-stricken threesome to keep their sense of family. The McCartneys' next-door neighbor, Tom Gall, also contributes a substantial share of care. He sometimes helps prepare Paul's and Mike's after-school meals. But when the after-school discussion turns to this new rock'n'roll sound, Gall and the older McCartney son don't concur. The next-door neighbor prefers classical music to this teenage ruckus.

The teenage Paul is a helter-skelter of raw emotions after his mother's death. The event sets an ocean liner of doubt adrift in the heretofore navigable waters of his life. In the midst of his daily pain, he tries to empathize with his father's and brother's pain. He also tries to erect a smoke screen of good cheer. But, inside, the sudden, final, total cutting of the umbilical cord is numbing. His emotions are ready to flake apart like dried blood at the slightest touch. The minutes and hours and days and weeks and months and years of the rest of his life seem to stretch endlessly ahead of him. The deep despondency could have been calamitous. But the teenager turns to the music of the day for solace—turns to rock for refuge.

The music had been an enjoyable if distant interest to him. But after his mother's death, the young man shifts his eyes and heart to rock'n'roll as if it's a lighthouse—a lighthouse in a storm—winking at him in the distance, or the green light at the end of Daisy's dock in *The Great Gatsby*. The music gives him hope—a ton of tonic for a grieving soul. Rock'n'roll—both listening to it and playing it—becomes his panacea. It helps him keep the grownup world's pain and boredom at bay; soothes his troubled mind. The sudden grief foments a sudden passion for rock'n'roll. As darkness passes over his inner horizons, there's a compensatory widening of those horizons. The teenager's father had been encouraging him for years to learn an instrument. He had bought him a trumpet for his birthday, but the youngster didn't stay with it. He had sent him to piano lessons, but the boy didn't seem interested. He had gotten him a tryout for the Liverpool Cathedral Choir, but the boy failed the audition.

Then, on November 11, 1956, with the skiffle fad in full flower, the fourteen-year-old McCartney saw Lonnie Donegan at the Liverpool Empire. He soon after decided he wanted to play the guitar. His father didn't particularly like this new rock'n'roll stuff, but he somehow dug up 15 pounds ($42) to buy a guitar for his son. The guitar has the word *Zenith* written in brown above the tuning pegs. The former bandleader uses the piano to teach his teenage son a few chords on his new instrument. From there on, for the young man, there is only the guitar. The father quickly realizes that the guitar is no toy to the boy. The feeling of the music is strong in him. He goes from liking music to loving it; from stirred up to all shook up. For James Paul, like James Bond, it's a matter of shaken, not stirred. Rock'n'roll becomes the greatest thing since bikes.

McCartney comes to be unswerving in his resolve to learn every tune he likes, from Elvis Presley and Little Richard on down. The teenager disciplines himself through many, many hours of guitar labor. He busts his nails, among other things, to learn the instrument. The guitar puts a full-Nelson on his time. He practices anytime, anyplace. Sometimes he practices in his bedroom, imitating his idols in front of the dresser mirror. Sometimes he performs the voice parts between classes at school. Sometimes he practices at home in the bathroom where his voice and guitar take on a hard-tiled resonance, and the ceiling paint is flaking. As the paint chips away from the ceiling, the teenage guitarist ignores it as he chips away in the concert halls of his imagination. At 18 Forthlin Road, Tom Gall can't understand why anyone would spend all those hours in a peeling-ceiling bathroom, roughing it in an atmosphere of rock'n'roll dandruff.

Wherever the young McCartney plays, there is a spiritual sequestering of self. The switchboard in his brain puts everyone on hold. He would no more open the door on what he's doing than a photographer would open the door while a picture is developing. As he beavers day and night on this wooden guitar wall around himself, his competence increases in quantum leaps. He's more charged than a cloud full of lightning.

The musician in him grows out of rapture and emotion, not career goals. It's not as if he thinks he has found something that will give him a good job some day. Unknown to him, his occupational quarry is in sight. But that's not why he's playing guitar this July of 1957. He has never been in a band and has no thoughts of joining one. He hasn't even given his first stage show, and won't until this August when he and his brother will enter a talent contest at a Butlin's Holiday Camp at Filey, Yorkshire.

In the main, what has the young Paul playing rock'n'roll has far more to do with adolescence than ambition. Like the teenager on Menlove Avenue, Woolton, he discovers himself pulling away from a dependence on adults to energize him—to show him the truth of reality. And, like Lennon, as he unplugs from the adult-dependent world, he plugs into rock'n'roll. The sound gives him escape from an adult world which has hurt him with death . . . and it gains him acceptance in a private teen world.

Rock'n'roll empowers the young man. The teenage Paul finds a creative nucleus in himself that no one can split or scratch or even touch. It becomes an important power because outside events do not seem to be in his control. The power allows him to separate himself from thoughts of events as they are . . . and to invent a world he wants. Whether it be a world of the future, of the present, or of yesterday, it will be *his* world; a teenage world; a world of his teenage music.

So it is that the older son of a former bandleader finds himself in his backyard strumming a guitar at age fifteen. Actually, he's *fourteen* regular years and *one* long, long, long year—the past eight months without his mother having toyed meanly with his inner clock. In the bedrock of his being, McCartney is fifteen . . . going on fifty. This afternoon the teenager's neck is wet with sweat. As he strums away the time, it crosses his mind that he's going to a garden party in Woolton today and will meet up with Ivan Vaughan there.

Vaughan is a classmate of McCartney's at the Liverpool Institute and was born on the exact same day as McCartney in June of '42. A bookish but impish young man, he is a neighbor and friend of John Lennon. Every now and again, he plays a tea chest bass in Lennon's group, the Quarry Men. Painted on the bass are the words, "Jive with Ive, the ace on the bass." Vaughan knows how much McCartney likes rock'n'roll, so he invited him to go to the fête and meet Lennon and his band. It took no goading to get him to go. But McCartney's prime reason for going is more hormones than harmonies: he hopes he might meet some girls there.

The teenage guitarist stops playing. He looks across the big Police College training field behind his yard. There are no police training at the moment; just kids playing. He watches them. His eyes are brown as the bark of a walnut tree. He looks up into the pearly glare of the sky over Allerton. It's hot and getting hotter. He gets up from the striped folding chair and guides his brown sandals into the house to see if the tea is ready.

Just about ready, by 1:49 P.M., is the St. Peter's Church fête procession through Woolton Village. The Liverpool police have blocked off streets for the parade route. The field behind St. Peter's is festooned with little colored flags and balloons and bunting. Tents and folding chairs and fair workers and early arrivals dot the big green clearing. Beribboning the field perimeter are stalls for a variety of games and goodies. In the heat, the area behind the church has the liquid layer of a mirage. Harry Forrest, the electrician turned fair organizer, walks across the field and mops the sweat from his brow.

On Church Road, five bedecked lorries await the Rose Queen and the Youth Club and the Brownies and the Quarry Men and all the other young people who will help to open the fête on a high note. Several youngsters, and some oldsters, mill around the big flatbed trucks. Some of the kids are still getting dressed in the church hall across the street. During these endmost preparations, the sun is a weight upon Liverpool. But it's all smiles on Church Road, Woolton, as people prepare for their day on the jazzed-up lorries and on the sweet-scented field. The smells and smiles and swelter form a blend that dusts the day with enchantment.

The stage is set.

EARLY AFTERNOON

John Lennon, sporting a seventh-heaven grin, stands on Church Road, Woolton, and stares bemusedly at the scenario before him. It's 1:56 P.M. The sixteen-year-old has drunk a quantity of alcohol. His breath is rich with beer. He's in a semidaze and his mind is trafficking in non-Euclidian patterns. His brain feels doughy. He has had a big-time argument this morning; he's hoping to have a good-time bash this afternoon. At the moment, the swelling summer heat is doing a foxtrot with his beer-head.

Now, in that frame of mind, he struggles to hold back outright laughter. His latest chore of the day is to climb up to the tailboard of a flatback coal lorry for the purpose of playing a guitar there. When all is said and done, that makes about as much sense to him as the heat and the drink and the argument. But the teenager knows the routine. So he goes with it. He ascends the big long lorry, gripping his guitar by the neck, and has himself a look-see. He lights a cigarette. He knows every cobblestone in Woolton, but he has never seen Church Road from this vantage point. He's with his band, the Quarry Men, on the last of the five flatbed trucks.

Amidst much teenage bantering, he cranes his neck and gapes down Church Road. He flicks some ashes and takes a drag on his cigarette. The streetscape has the touch of a dream to young Lennon. The early afternoon itself is far from a dream. It's autumn gray and summer humid. A British bullfinch darts through the 79-degree heat. He alights on a big gnarled elm tree. Once in a while, the sun peeps through the gray-browed clouds. The sky furnishes a bleak frame for the pictures in Lennon's tightly squinted eyes.

The sideburned musician peers down the lane and samples a homemade stew of bright impressions. It's as if the scene has been dabbed with Halloween torches. His eyes aren't sharp enough to tell that the faces are eager, but he knows other things. The mood is festive. Hearts are light. Talk is loose. Colors rage. Half a dozen kids are dressed up like little soldiers in white caps and red jackets and white sashes. The soon-to-be-crowned 1957 Rose Queen strolls past Lennon. She is thirteen-year-old Sally Wright and she looks silken in her white lace gown and her train of pink velvet. A hive of kids gather around the queen bee as she heads for the lead-off lorry. She takes her seat, her back to the cab, under a flower-bedecked trellis that curves like a rose-filled rainbow over her head. There's a folded-up raincoat and an umbrella by her feet, just in case.

From near the front of the procession comes the fat, brassy sound of the Band of the Cheshire Yeomanry. The twenty-five-man military band will escort the procession through town. Proudly draped in their big-lapeled, navy-blue uniforms, they run through the opening notes of several marching tunes. Midway down the processional queue of parked lorries, a troop of Morris Dancers loosens up. The Morris Dancers, like the military band, will not ride on the big trucks. In their bright white pompom-capped shoes, they'll leap their way through the Woolton streets this afternoon. At the very front of the Church Road caravan is the fête secretary, Henry Hilditch. He stands with his hands clasped behind his back and waits for a signal to start.

At the back, the Quarry Men founder takes in the images from what feels to him like a bird's-eye view. He takes a last drag on his cigarette and flicks it away. There is an air of band fraternity on the fifth and final truck. The team of gangly teenagers called the Quarry Men Skiffle Group is having fun. Lennon notices the fair organizer, Harry Forrest, rushing toward the front of the parade while giving a fast answer to the ten-thousandth obvious question he has been asked this day.

The St. Peter's Church clock rings 2 P.M. The marching band and the fleet of lorries sally forth down Church Road—as if this is how it has been done since time immemorial. You get the feeling that this is just how it is in the Liverpool village: in the winter, you take down glassy Christmas tree decorations and remember other winters; in the summer, you walk across the grassy, well-treed field and remember other summers. It's a way of beating time . . . in both hot and cold weather.

Fête secretary Hilditch wears an air of high office as he leads the way with wide swings of a mace—a ceremonial club with an ornament at the top. The route goes left from Church Road onto Allerton Road, right onto Woolton Street, left down Kings Drive, right onto Hunt's Cross Avenue, up Manor Road, onto Speke Road, and then back into Woolton Street, Allerton Road, and Church Road. The sun inches its way across a vault of cataract-colored sky. Every time there is a brightening, someone in the procession turns a sun-shaded face upward. The parade almost seems to float in the heat. En route to absolutely nowhere, the younger kids sit with their feet dangling off the edges of the big trucks. The Brownies and Cubs and children in costumes enjoy the bouncy ride.

From opposite sides of the streets, Woolton homes smile across at one another showing windowpanes as high gloss as well-kept teeth. The military band sends its brassy beat boomeranging off the quaint old Woolton structures. The band keeps the pace slow and the mood up. Bobbies in their chin-strapped black helmets detain traffic at intersections to let the parade pass. The Morris Dancers twirl their streamer-tipped batons. The pompoms on their white shoes flit like giant white flies across the Woolton lanes. On the tailboard of the first lorry, Sally Wright, local Rose Queen, smiles and tries to preen and wishes that someone would stroke the sweat off her forehead with a cool cloth.

The crowds bulge at curbside to watch the parading

merrymakers. There are grownups and teens and children
and baby carriages. One boy on Kings Drive regards the
proceedings from his father's shoulders. While the parade
worms forward, St. Peter's Youth Club members are on
foot, collecting money. They keep abreast of the procession and hold out cans with coin slits on top. Most people
make a donation.

Getting a full gaze from the teenagers at curbside is
the last of the lorries—the one motorvating with the
Quarry Men Skiffle Group on it. The youngsters are be-
wildered that a teenage band is in the parade. They
couldn't be more discombobulated if the lorry were a di-
nosaur with a Tolkien dwarf on its back. This kind of
adult recognition of their music is unheard-of, almost
freakish.

Conversely, some grownups hear the band and wish
they hadn't put their winter earmuffs away. They receive
the din lightly—just some teen thing that will be old hat
by tomorrow. Lorry number five, in the meantime, serves
up a jangling acoustic sound on a big long plate of high-
pitched jocularity. While playing their songs, the teenagers verbally fence with each other, rubber tips on their
words. The bandleader, in particular, wields his wit.

An open palm of breeze catches Lennon's painstakingly
combed hair and touches his beer-warm cheeks. He enjoys
the pocket-sized chill. More than that, he enjoys the fact
that he and his band are getting to play out for people.
Since starting the band in March, the teenage guitarist
has made a bold effort to hook his group up with local
audiences. But the band has not exactly gained a toehold

on the international music scene. Its engagements have been mostly dances, competitions, parties. The group's first official performance was less than a month ago, June 9, at Liverpool's Empire Theatre. The Quarry Men did an audition that afternoon for a television show called *TV Star Search*, but they didn't make the cut. The band's only other large-attraction engagement has been an outdoor show on June 22, when they played from the tailboard of a stationary coal lorry on Rosebery Street in Liverpool. The occasion was a block party that was part of the yearlong celebration of Liverpool's gaining its charter 750 years ago.

The teenage band is no great shakes this early July afternoon. But they're having a good time. The "Quarry Men" moniker comes from the fact that most of the bandmates go to Quarry Bank Grammar School. Lennon had first discussed the idea of a group with his buddy Pete Shotton, who teamed up with Lennon out of friendship, not musicianship. The wiry-haired Shotton plays a washboard obtained from a shed in his garden.

Eric Griffiths, a young man with the eyes of a young hawk, enlists with the Quarry Men on guitar. Colin Hanton combines his job as an apprentice upholsterer in a factory with his job at the hot seat as the group's drummer. A top-level Quarry Bank student named Rod Davis brings his Windsor Whirle banjo to the small-whirl troupe. The lean-physiqued Len Garry focuses his talents on the homemade instrument called the tea chest bass. A tea chest is a square box made out of plywood and used for transporting tea. This packing case is turned into a musical instrument by stretching a long string from it to the top of a broom-handle-size rod. The rod is freestanding. Moving it has the effect of tightening or slackening the string, producing a deeper or higher sound when the string is plunked. Lennon's friend Ivan Vaughan sometimes lends a hand on tea chest bass, but not today. The group's original tea chest bass player had been a Quarry Bank schoolmate named Bill Smith. Another Lennon friend, Nigel Whalley, is the band's manager.

Of the six Quarry Men on the parade lorry this afternoon, four wear white cotton shirts with collars. Only Lennon and his tea chest bassist, Len Garry, have colored shirts. As the parade sashays forward, the teenage bandleader begins to tire of standing mannequinlike on a mobile stage. He had played on one of these big trucks at Rosebery Street the other day, but that truck didn't move. Today, the moving truck is throwing him off stride. He feels as if he's not really playing for anybody, because they only hear him for a few seconds and then he's out of earshot. The absence of real listeners destroys his desire to play. It's one thing to sit on your bed at home and have no one hear you play. But this is supposed to be playing for people. It seems fake to him.

The sixteen-year-old Lennon stands on the big truck, guitar in his hands, and feels like a comical figure as the truck drives on. How can anyone appreciate his music if, by the time they hear a couple of seconds of it, he's gone? He gets his band to play a little rock'n'roll; taps into his spiritual pipeline. But even that doesn't make it worth it. On the big floating platform, his feet feel unreal, as if they've been shot through with novacaine. Finally, he despairs of playing. He puts his guitar down and spends the rest of his truck-guided sightseeing tour joshing with his friends.

The five lorries pull up to Church Road to unload their precious cargo. It's 2:51 P.M. The procession of time is far swifter than the procession of Woolton. Several men on Church Road help the children alight from the lorries. The older kids clamber off. The younger kids look like costumed frogs hopping off lorry lilies. From Church Road, the Band of the Cheshire Yeomanry guides the parade through the narrow passageway next to the church. The band blares a brassy trail from the footpath to the fairground. Firstcomers on the field applaud the entrance of the procession through the gates. Standing at the gate working admission duty are the short, shrill-voiced John Moorst and his assistant, Fred Toakley, a stout, gravel-voiced fellow. The gatekeepers balance one another as they collect money and check programs. Admission is 6 pence for adults, 3 pence for children. The fête program, which has been sold during the week, serves as an admission ticket.

The military band marches mightily past the gatekeepers and takes a slow lap around the church field. The band serenades the crowd sonorously, punctuating its repertoire with lots of drumrolls. The people sit in folding chairs or stand about and watch and applaud. No one works the stalls or sideshows until after the Rose Queen's coronation. The queen and her royal juvenile legion wend their way down the footpath onto the church field. They're followed by the rest of the afternoon's lorry commuters, including the little local teen pop group called the Quarry Men. The band carries its equipment onto the upper part of the field and stores it in the long, wooden scouts' hut. The hut has a barracks feel to it. Some scouts are in there, playing their bugles. The musicians of the Quarry Men leave the hut to see what kind of female flowers are blooming at the garden party.

By four minutes to three, the military band has stopped playing and gone off on break. The 1957 Rose Queen, thirteen-year-old Miss Wright, sits in the middle of a bunting-strung stage on the big green field. Sitting up there with her are various church and fête officials. The stage is a wooden platform just shy of three feet high with stairs on both sides. The entire platform measures about twenty-five feet wide and fifteen feet deep. A couple of posts behind either side of the stage support wire netting. The netting has tree branches hanging on it as a decorative summery backdrop. At the rear corners of the platform are holly and beech-tree boughs propped up by bricks. At the front corners of the platform hang British flags. At stage center there's a bulky microphone with mesh on it. The mike is hooked up with a couple of old gray horn speakers at the sides of the stage. It's a basic public address system.

The rain-washed church field is dry. It's 3:03 P.M. The bespectacled rector of St. Peter's Church, Reverend Morris Pryce Jones, steps up to the microphone. He's a big man with owlish eyes and large hands and an outgoing personality. He starts to talk, and there's a groan of distortion from the P.A. system. He tries again. It's all right this time. The rector says a prayer and welcomes the crowd. Thence come the highlighting ceremonials of this royal picnic. Reverend Pryce Jones introduces Mrs. Thelwall Jones, the woman who will do the crowning. Framed by tree branches on a church field, teenager Sally Wright accedes to her rule of the dream-dusted day. Mrs. Jones places the gold foil crown on Miss Wright's brushed, light brown hair. Her young majesty feels goose flesh run wildly across her back. The gathering cheers politely. When she's handed a bouquet, the young lady seems like a modern-day Cinderella—with a lorry for a pumpkin coach, a foil crown for a glass slipper, and the final second of July 6, 1957, for her stroke of midnight.

But until that moment, Woolton, Liverpool, will have two queens . . . and one of them is a teenager. The queen for a day tosses her crowned head back with innocent panache. Her royal subjects applaud. Reverend Pryce Jones wipes his sweaty forehead with a handkerchief as he inconspicuously leaves the stage. At 4:08 P.M. there is one more piece of protocol before the fair is declared open, the fancy-dress parade and competition. Dozens of children march around in assumed identities. There is a nurse and a clown and a Hawaiian girl and a sewing box and Little Red Riding Hood. Four children dress up to represent the four seasons. There are, as usual, many soldiers. The very little soldiers march very out of step.

After about twenty minutes prizes are given, there is a smattering of applause, and the fête is declared open. The teen queen steps off the stage and mingles with her friends. Dozens of men and women go to their stalls and sideshows. The military band cranks up the brass again. Kids flock in all directions.

The fun has begun.

In St. Peter's Church, next to the day's fairground, an insurance inspector named Noel Morrison is marrying a shorthand typist named Barbara Broadhurst. The bride's headdress has orange blossoms in it. The church organ sends the Liverpool couple off to a hundred person reception at the Gateacre Country Club.

The major horse race of the Liverpool day is off at 3:18 P.M. It's the Old Newton Cup at Haydock Park. Winning the race by half a length is Rhythmic Light. In no hurry at all to win anything this afternoon is the Mersey River—that brooding river of passing time—nor are its daily workmates. A ferryboat loafs across the river in the mounting heat.

In other outdoor activities—outside of Liverpool—this afternoon, A. D. Abbot-Anderson wins the British Army Rifle Championship at Bisley in Surrey. The twenty-year-old senior under-officer is the best of the hundred marksmen who made it to the finals.

In Wimbledon tennis today, Althea Gibson of New York becomes the first black person to win a Wimbledon singles title. She defeats Darlene Hard of Montebello, California, 6–3, 6–2. Queen Elizabeth attends the finals and congratulates Gibson, saying, "It must have been very hot out there." The match also marks the first time that Wimbledon has ever had a demonstration. A woman dressed completely in white runs toward center court and unfolds a banner which reads: SAVE OUR QUEEN. She starts to parade the banner around and to shout, but is whisked away expeditiously. She says later, "The taxpayer demands an honest banking charter to kill war today." The demonstration rends the occasion's refined ambience.

In the United States this afternoon, the Harry S Truman Library is dedicated in Independence, Missouri. Among the two thousand people at the ceremony are former Presidents Truman and Herbert Hoover, as well as Mrs. Franklin D. Roosevelt. Chief Justice Earl Warren delivers the keynote address in front of the limestone and marble building. The library is the fourth of its kind in the U.S.A. and will store Truman's official papers, personal mementos, and assorted memorabilia. Meanwhile, down in Memphis, Tennessee, Mrs. Don Thompson turns on the garden hose to fill the plastic swimming pool she won at a raffle in her rural neighborhood. The hose has run an hour and a half when she notices that the pool isn't nearly filled. Upon investigation she ascertains that the pool holds twelve thousand gallons of water, and that filling it would take three days and all the water from every well in her neighborhood.

On Lime Street in Liverpool, England, there's a golden-rimmed clock on the front of a capacious tavern. The place is called Peter Walker's Vines—more popularly known as the Vines. The clock on the Vines says 3:38 P.M. In the Liverpool suburb of Woolton, teenage bandleader John W.

Lennon saunters through a church fairground. He feels hot and sticky. The Liverpool day continues to work sedulously at burning itself out. An occasional sun falls with affable affection upon the young man's face.

His first salutation from the church field is the bakery smell. Breathing tastes good. He notices how the odors commingle with the smell of summer, and the effect is almost dizzying. An odd feeling of homesickness steals over the teenager—odd because he *is* home. It's as if he's mulling over the memories of his boyhood . . . and finding them a trifle distant. Without thinking, he rubs the heels of his hands into his eyes.

The eyes scan the panorama. The tents make the church field look like a trading post on a long green meadow borrowed from North Dakota. Little V-shaped colored flags snap in the slight southeasterly breeze. The young man looks across the field and thinks. He's unmindful of today's date and of the fact that July 6 is the day in Ernest Hemingway's *The Sun Also Rises* when the fiesta begins in Pamplona, Spain. In the novel, July 6 is the first day of the annual, week-long fiesta of San Fermin, which blends religious ritual with fireworks and the running of the bulls through city streets. There are no bulls running through the streets of Woolton this July 6. In their small-town feast, the people are experiencing other joys.

Throughout the so-fine afternoon, the village fête cajoles its denizens and visitors with food and fun and, most copiously of all, friendship. The event is out-of-doors, but the feeling is homey. An at-ease smile surfaces on the young guitarist's face as he makes the rounds of stalls and sideshows. Up and down the sides of the field there are a couple of dozen stalls. They sell cakes and fruits and vegetables and sweets and books. There is a white elephant stall chock full of things that are of no use to their previous owners, but might fetch a shilling for the church if deemed useable by somebody else. The Sunday School runs a grocery stall. The Brownies and Girl Guides sell soft drinks. The Mothers Union corners the fairground fashion market with a haberdashery stall.

It's 3:47 P.M. He's no child anymore, but the sideburned Lennon has a go at most of the game stalls. The games have names like Treasure Hunt and Shilling-in-the-Bucket and Bagatelle and Hoopla. The box-office success of the afternoon is the balloon stall. A balloon is filled with hydrogen at your request. You write your name and address on a card which is attached to the balloon. Then you let the balloon fly away. The one discovered farthest from the church field will win a prize.

Another hot stop at the fête is the Honest Jack dartboard by the right side of the stage. The "Jack" refers not to the game, but to the fellow who runs it: Jack Gibbons, the St. Peter's Youth Club Director. A tall man with a sunshiny face, he kindles a feeling of cheer in the local kids. He made the dartboard in 1950. The board is eight feet wide and five feet deep and has the fifty-two cards of a deck tacked to it. You get three darts for three pence. You win if you hit three cards. The better the combination of cards, the better the prize. . . . About the only thing missing to make the fair a full-fledged carnival is a professional fire-eater—which they could use to their advantage, with the heat being what it is.

The fête is less than an hour underway and the crowd already numbers in the hundreds. The scene is a symphony of symmetry: everything is harmonious. The kids, especially, are jubilant. The game stalls are choked with young people, who are also enjoying the low-priced refreshments. The kids run and laugh and jump. They're in full robustness. The summer weather gives them a sweet, open feeling of freedom.

Feeling just as free, but displaying it at a lower decibel level, the Woolton grownups maintain an unremitting flow of chitchat. The conversation bounces back and forth across the field like the tennis balls at Reynolds Park. There are a few babies in their mothers' arms. The hawking of cakes and the cries of laughter mix with the marches and light music played by the Band of the Cheshire Yeomanry. The group's roped off, curving row of folding chairs on the field is to the left of the stage. Many people try to get near the band so that they can hear them better. There is a dampness along the tops of the military uniform collars. One of the band members lifts a navy blue sleeve and glances at his wristwatch. He feels that it's time for a break, and he knows that the program has the teenage skiffle group scheduled to come on at 4:15.

It's five past four. Teenager John Lennon gathers his bandmates into the scouts' hut on the upper field. They get their equipment and get ready. About a mile away, in the

Liverpool suburb of Allerton, teenager Paul McCartney is also getting ready. He stands in front of a bathroom mirror and combs his hair. He squeezes one more pearl of Brylcream into his right hand and runs it through his scalp. The teen sweeps the thick, dark brown hair up and back. It stands up high in front. He goes into his bedroom and drapes a long, white sports jacket across his shoulders. The jacket is a rock'n'roll fashion footnote to a popular song, Marty Robbins's "A White Sport Coat and a Pink Carnation." The young McCartney doesn't have any pink carnations in the house or garden, so he settles for his jacket having pocket flaps and light speckles and wide lapels.

The teenage guitarist is making the most of the fact that he can wear what he wants today. Since it's a Saturday, he can jettison his school blazer and white shirt and tie. He's particularly proud of his black slacks. They're about as narrow as the drainpipe that runs down the back of his Forthlin Road home. He takes a last look at his hair and picks up his guitar and heads outside. It's the same kind of warm day as the one that, four years ago in 1953, the McCartneys became the first on the block to own a television. The family had spent that summer day watching Queen Elizabeth II's coronation.

Without forethought, McCartney straps the guitar on his back, gets on his bike and starts for the Woolton fête. He negotiates the uphill ride with enthusiasm. The teenage McCartney is large eyed as he leans over the handlebars. His head swirls with riotous summer dreams. He grips the handlebars irremovably—the same way he grips the guitar when he plays. His black-slacked legs work the power of his three-speed, drop-head Raleigh.

The bicycle zips over the Liverpool streets and roads and the Allerton Municipal Golf Course, which bisects the Lennon and McCartney homes. Now and then, the bike's chrome shoots sun arrows through the nebulous heat. In his long, white jacket, fifteen-year-old Paul gleams with youth as he crosses over Menlove Avenue. The hot afternoon makes the jacket look Arctic white. It fluffs up around him like a miniature bridal train.

LATE AFTERNOON

The air has thickened. The rising southeasterly breeze stirs the church field trees into rustling conversation. Overhead, a couple of soft vanilla sailboats wage a losing battle with several gray battleships. Every once in a while, there's a brilliant flash of sunshine.

Ten past four now.

With the swelling humidity, the Woolton garden party goes through cups and glasses by the crate. The biggest aid of the day turns out to be lemonade. The drink and food are plentiful. The fête is in full flame. The church grassland is jammed with several hundred bodies. The faces are gladsome and the faces are sweaty. Many handkerchiefs flutter from many purses and dab many drops of sweat. It's as if the air has no breathing room in it.

There's a wide swatch of the local Liverpool population—a varicose vein for every fresh face. The place is jammed with skylarking kids. Vivaciousness runs high.

No one on the fairground wishes to be a hundred miles away, or a hundred feet, or even down the lane. There is the buzz of conversation and the brass of the marching band. The mood of the moment is rhapsodic. In that mindset, the people might not notice anything even if you were to replant them on the San Andreas Fault and there was a buckling sound.

To the kids, the fair has become a contest of sorts: who can eat the most, win the most, take part in the most events the most number of times. The kids are inordinately clamorous around a children's event called the Aerial Run. Concocted by some Woolton Boy Scouts, it operates along a twenty-foot-high rope that stretches from the upper field to the lower field. The rope has pulleys attached to a little chair harness.

A light-haired nine-year-old boy, after waiting on line almost ten minutes, is buckled into the chair from a small platform on the upper field. With a quick shove, the chair is sent sliding down the long slope. The ride picks up speed and the boy's jaw drops low and fast, as if his chin were made of taffy and someone had just yanked it hard. He gets off the ride on the lower field. He's breathing in rapid rasps and he's grinning. Emboldened by his successful shuttle flight, he trots back to the upper field to get on line again. It's the next best thing to a rocking horse with wings.

The ride is carefully supervised by adults. Even more carefully supervised is the open sandstone quarry that borders the church field. The quarry is a giant reddish tooth gap in the mouth of smiling Woolton. Using pickaxes and dynamite, men work the site daily, cutting the stone and taking it into town: quarry men. The riches of the excavation provided the stone for many Liverpool churches, ranging from Woolton's St. Peter's Church on up to the Anglican cathedral. Many Liverpool homes and schools were also mined from the Woolton site.

By 1957, the sides of the quarry amount to a steep cliff. There's a stone wall built where the quarry skirts the church field. Then there's a fence in front of the wall. Even so, throughout the fête this afternoon, there are several men keeping guard by the fence. Their only job is to walk back and forth in front of the fence and make sure that no children go over it. The scene is suggestive of the central image in a novel by J. D. Salinger called *The Catcher in the Rye*. Published in 1951, the work is beginning to reach a much larger audience this year because of the recent boom in paperback books. *The Catcher in the Rye* takes its title from the role the main character, Holden Caulfield, imagines for himself. In the story, he evokes an image of a bunch of kids playing in a field of rye that borders on a cliff. He imagines himself having the job of standing on the edge of the cliff and catching the kids before they fall off.

It's 4:15 P.M.—time to go from the brass band to the brash band; time for the band with the guitarist who spends hours a day digging through a musical rock quarry with his bare hands; time for the wild card in the afternoon's entertainment deck to step up to the wooden scaffold. The Quarry Men—the musical ones, that is—are onstage and ready to be introduced. They're scheduled to play from 4:15 to 4:45. At 4:45, the military band is due back on. There's a dog show at 5:15. Then the Quarry Men are to come back on at 5:45. They're also slated to play the dance later in the evening at the church hall across the street.

By 4:15 the Quarry Men bandleader has a slight wheeling feeling from the beers that slid down his throat earlier. His argument with his aunt this morning now seems like something out of the far distant past. He's looking forward to playing for the home folks. It's no big thing to him—just a good workout of his young rock'n'roll muscles. He wonders if he can turn the fair mood from rocking horse to rocking—if he can turn the little upcountry outdoor platform into a bandstand.

On the bandstand with him are his band brothers and the equipment they've carried over from the scouts' hut. Near the center of the stage, to the right of the microphone, is the two-foot-square tea chest bass. It's painted black, and on the front it has a silver treble clef and musical notes kicking up their heels. The entire square black box is trimmed in silver. The other standout piece of stage impedimenta is the bass drum toward the back of center stage. It has the appellation QUARRY MEN splashed in big black letters across the middle. The bass drum also has the drummer's name, in smaller letters, printed at the top of it: COLIN HANTON.

As they wait onstage to be introduced, the Quarry Men comprise a gaggle of six bouncing boys, sleeves rolled up, ready to rock: John Lennon, singer and guitar player, holding securely onto a dark brown acoustic that's be-fringed in white; Eric Griffiths, guitarist, who keeps on the lookout for Lennon's next move; Len Garry, tea chest bassist, who is feeling hot already and opens the top button of his plaid shirt; Colin Hanton, drummer, whose ruminative eyes roam the audience from behind his Broadway drum kit; Pete Shotton, washboard player, whose blond hair is burnished by the off-again-on-again sunlight; and Rod Davis, banjo player, who is shifting from foot to foot as he looks through his glasses at the fête gathering.

The clock set in the old sandstone tower of St. Peter's Church says 4:17. The military band squelches itself into silence and the St. Peter's Church rector introduces the Quarry Men Skiffle Group. A young man with a guitar steps into the northern England country portrait.

He has a look in his eyes.

Teenager John Lennon weaves toward the glistening conical microphone that snakes out of the wooden scaffold. He stands stage center and looks across the afternoon. The audience senses immediately that he has a prepossessing presence, especially for one so young. Since he won't wear his glasses and he's in a pint-sized alcohol fog, he looks through a hazy lens at the hazy day. His weak eyesight is filtered through a yellow gauze of beer. To him, the people look like bands of confetti pendulating across a big lawn. He says hello and introduces the band. The sound carries clearly through the two gray horn speakers. The voice gives the feeling of a summer breeze with a pungent sea-spray in it.

The band breaks into its first song. They dispense a shower of notes into the humid sticky air. It is a rusty, ringing sound. The notes bounce off the nearby gravestones of Liverpool dead; rocket up into the low Liverpool sky. Near the front of the stage, a toothless baby in her mother's arms lets out a lengthy squeal. A fat, tan squirrel scurries from under the stage and into the trees behind. The young music snaps the quaint mood of the fair; shreds the tapestry of the gentle afternoon into vibrant teen threads. The surf of sound rolls over the entire field and washes through every pair of eardrums.

The audience picks up the trip-hammer thunder. It grabs the people out of various attitudes of distraction. Mouths stop. Eyebrows raise. Feet start shuffling in the direction of the bandstand. The first thought in many people's minds is that the P.A. system has gone wacko. After all, who in the Woolton world would trigger such a racket at a church-related event? And right next to the church no less! This is not the sort of thing that drifts gracefully out of the St. Peter's Church choirstalls. The incongruity is staggering. It's as if the sound has jumped out of the speakers and beaten up the vicar.

It takes a few seconds to begin to place understanding between the fact of what is happening and the comprehension of it. After the initial shock, the first comprehension for many is that, while they don't know what the banging is about, it sounds cheerful. Among those attempting to comprehend the sound are the singer's birth mother, his aunt Mimi, and two other aunts of his. The two aunts and his mother are pleased and proud to see the teenager up on the stage. His aunt Mimi—his aunt-guardian-mother—is another story. When the Quarry Men hit their first note, she had been on the upper field in the big white refreshment tent. She had emerged from the tent, with several others, at the first crack of the rock'n'roll rumble.

Now she gazes across the green-belted church field. Her eyes buttonhole the young man with a guitar. For a moment, she is dumbstruck, because she hadn't known that her charge was in a band, or that he would be doing some kind of entertainment at the fête. It's as if someone has painted her nephew's face over another face in a photograph. The aunt turns flour white for a few seconds. It occurs to her that the teenager is out of her control and is going to do what he wants, no matter what she says or does.

She ferrets through the attentive assemblage and hovers near the rim of the stage. The teenage Lennon spots her. He unsmiles. For a millisecond, he feels like leaving the stage. Instead, he starts singing about her coming toward him, making up his own words to fit the tune he's doing. The young guitarist realizes that he has played himself into a corner. The elderly aunt stares. Her eyes are inquisitorial.

The throng in front of the stage had been magnetized within seconds of the singer saying hello. It's composed mainly of young people. They hearken to the sound. While Lennon's guitar gently tweaks, his band confreres rev into a good pace. The group is loud, but not abrasive. They hammer out a variety of skiffle and rock'n'roll tunes such as "Cumberland Gap" and "Maggie Mae" and "Be-Bop-a-Lula." Tiny spheroids of perspiration materialize on the Quarry Men's foreheads. The band chugs along like a Liverpool tug in shallow waters.

There is applause between songs and it encourages the ensemble. Lennon hears the applause and forges a smile that curls up at the ends like little whiskers. Most teenagers enjoy the band. Many adults and children don't care one way or the other. If there are any Quarry Bank schoolteachers at the fête, they must be wondering how this A-Number-One troublemaker ingratiated himself into playing at this event. No teacher could picture this young man being able to do serious business with any adult. Yet, here he is, in the middle of the day's position of honor, right where a coronation has taken place—the Rose Queen supplanted by the thorn in the side.

For some other adults, the band's music is a matter of taste, and they don't like the taste of it. They believe that the Quarry Men would do better for themselves, and for society at large, if they were to trade in their musical instruments for pickaxes and become real quarry men. Just the same, there are many other adults who don't necessarily care for the music but feel that the young sound confers a sanguine blessing on the day's deeds.

Evidently, most members of the community do not regard the music as an infliction upon them. Testament to that is the very fact of the teen band being allowed to play this afternoon. Rather, most adults accept the music as novel and fun and lively—the stuff of youth. It's the same kind of youth-accommodating spirit that gave a Liverpool fellow who was only in his early twenties the opportunity to design the architectural wonder known as St. George's Hall, on Lime Street. It is an edifice of grandeur. Sixteen Corinthian columns give an ancient aura to the hall itself. The lampposts on the expansive promenade manifest dolphins carved into the bases in fine detail. In front of the entire magnificent design, verging on the street, are stone statues of four lions. The lions are in a crouching position. They look ready to pounce.

It's 4:28 P.M. About ten minutes into the Quarry Men show, the high-spirited, high-haired teenager from Allerton, Paul McCartney, arrives on his bike at the church field. He leans the bike against a fence. The cologne of freshly baked cakes grazes his nose. There is a moderate breeze. The afternoon sky is toneless. The sun gilds the area every few minutes. The teenager wonders about the music he's hearing. It's definitely not standard fare for a church fair, at least no church fair that he has ever been to.

McCartney walks into the big open field. In today's *Liverpool Echo*, this is the teenage John Lennon's Libra horoscope: "All sorts of things come into the open today." The horoscope continues: "The whole week is good for learning where you stand and how you can best achieve your aims. A little quiet thinking out will be all to the good."

McCartney walks through the field desultorily. He's not even aware of the guitar strapped to his back; it's like a body part. In the sun, his hair seems to have brown lights in it. The Liverpool earth receives his shadow warmly.

The teenager's gaze is all over the place at once. The big brown eyes sweep the big green pasturage. His attention bounces around the fair like a glinting silver ball in a pinball machine. He hits a few bumpers, rings a few bells, picks up glimmers from the area of the stage as the band's equipment dispatches half a dozen little suns. Near the middle of the field he sees his friend Ivan Vaughan. McCartney goes over to Vaughan, a dark-haired young man with an ever-ready smile. They greet and Vaughan nods toward the music. The two of them walk over to the left side of the stage.

They shoulder their way forward until there are only a few yards of hot Liverpool aerosphere between the teenager named Lennon and the teenager named McCartney. Directly behind the trees behind Lennon is a church called St. Mary's. It's partially visible through open slashes in the trees. There is a priest at the church by the name of Father McKenzie. Lennon is singing a song called "Come Go with Me" by a five-man U.S. vocal group known as the Del Vikings. The song is the Del Vikings' first hit. It charts as high as Number 4 in America. They recorded the song in Pittsburgh while they were stationed at a local air force base. One of the air force musicians backing the group on the record is a drummer named Sgt. Peeples.

Paul McCartney, age fifteen, stands stock-still on the warm grass. He's as immobile as the black tuxed figure on the top of a wedding cake. It's 4:32 P.M. The air is toasty. The teenager hitches his thumbs in the pockets of his tight black pants. In his white jacket, he looks like one of his father's pipe cleaners sticking halfway out of a dark tobacco pouch. The wide round face turns to Lennon and locks in: a rock'n'roll radar dish picking up a signal. His eyes, not quite tea-saucer size, are transfixed on the stage. He stares intently. McCartney's brown diamond eyes mirror two John Lennons skating across their ice-watery surfaces.

He unhitches one thumb from a pocket and raises an open hand to his forehead to shield his eyes against a sudden sluice of sun. Like a sky-sailing wheel of fortune, the sun has displayed many different numbers this day, shown many different faces. The teenager's eyes land on Lennon's fingers. He fastens his mind on the guitar player at the microphone. The rest of the band—and the world —melt into the hot afternoon. His own feeling for rock'n'roll provides a musical drawbridge for him to cross the moat into Lennon's dream castle. McCartney puts the day's heat somewhere else: his facial features are frozen. Even his long-fringed eyelashes are motionless. He squints to the point where his eyebrows have a beetling cast.

The sleek, slender, slippery figure of sixteen-year-old John Lennon inclines his head toward the microphone and rips the local latitude and longitude with "Come Go with Me." He has a whipcord of a voice. This being his home field, he gives the show a little something extra. He purrs the lyric, then snarls it. The simple amplification system translates the lyric into bolts of words. In the long sculpture of his face, his mouth seems chiseled with a toenail cutter. His lips slice the words thin. The expression is half smile, half smirk.

The teenager doesn't know all the words to the song, so he makes some of them up. No one in the Quarry Men is surprised. His bandmates never know what he's going to do next when he picks up a guitar. He might do anything—and it will probably be fun. In his hands, the guitar is an exclamation point. Most of the audience doesn't know he's making up the words. Even most of the teenagers don't know it: they *hear* the lyrics, but they *understand* the drums and guitars. Besides, the singer knows how the song *feels*. He's getting that across, and that's what matters most.

With the start of each song, Lennon leaves Liverpool and lives in the music. He is nowhere but in the music. His legs are planted on the wooden scaffold; locks of hair hang over his forehead—locks to the front door of a rock'n'roll sweatshop. Adrenal sparks shoot through his back and calves and thighs. But his mind is in a castle of dreams; a velvety vertigo.

The intense, shifting, nonconformist actions of Lennon's life give form to the movement of his music. His guitar lines pour over the length of the grounds in a thin stream of silvery coins. He plays hard. To do less would be unconscionable to him. He loves the music that much. The hands are sturdy. The fingers are sure. He coils his left hand around the guitar neck in a grip like Queen Victoria's around the reins of her horse in front of St. George's Hall. This most proper of queens wouldn't approve of him at this moment, however, as he is patently not being proper; that is, he has a guitar in his hands, yet he's playing banjo chords, using only four strings. But he makes do. In a hot moment, he brandishes the guitar in the manner of a teenage toreador. In a cool moment, the guitar rocks back and forth like a grandfather clock's pendulum. In all moments, the Lennon guitar takes a beating. His first guitar had a label on the inside that said "Guaranteed Not to Split." This is his second guitar, a better one, but Rod Davis, next to him on banjo, wouldn't be surprised if it split any second.

As Lennon plays, he tries to take the crowd's pulse—tries to put his finger on what sorts of performer actions get what sorts of audience reactions. The light terra-cotta eyes window-shop across the multifarious English faces. The young guitarist offers a mixed bag of movements and gestures . . . and even expressions. In a single minute, his eyes stray from convivial to condemnatory to contemplative to convulsed—and back to convivial. Never do they look confused. He knows what he wants to be doing, and he's doing it.

In turn, some in the audience take *his* measure. There is a vertiginous sense about the singer-guitarist of both friendship and danger; of open fields and dark alleys; of a swishing blade of meadow and a switchblade. All that anyone can tell for sure about the young Lennon is that he's working up a good sweat—the war paint of the rock musician. A patch of sweat stains the back of his shirt. His onstage heart is a heavy hammer. His mouth is spitless. He swipes his lower lip with his tongue.

The teenager is having fun. He's having a rock'n'roll field day on the big Liverpool field.

A small shred of grass away, both thumbs in the corners of his peg-legged pants pockets, another teenager is also having fun. Fifteen-year-old guitarist Paul McCartney listens for a rock'n'roll heartbeat; looks down Lennon's throat for inflammation of the lyric. He finds the older teenager's health to be solid as a rock. This may be a garden party, but McCartney can tell that the guitar player is not garden variety.

In frisking Lennon's technical knowledge, he follows the guitarist's fingers and deciphers the fact that he's playing banjo chords. In taking an inventory of Lennon's singing background, he can tell that Lennon doesn't know all the words to all the songs. The young man makes note of and accepts these limitations. But, laserlike, he transpierces the limitations—sees past the banjo chords and wrong words and comes up with other perceptions.

To start with, Lennon's creative extemporaneousness etches itself across McCartney's mind. He likes how Lennon makes up words on the spot—suffuses the music with a teenage Liverpool touch. In addition, without even knowing all the words, the guy still captures the triumph of each song.

Secondly, the fifteen-year-old is taken by the concrete actuality of the band—the simple fact of its existence in the real world. Here's a cluster of local blokes—around his own age—up on a stage playing not-half-bad rock'n'roll.

And thirdly, McCartney realizes that, for the first time

in his life, he's looking at someone who cares about this crazy new music as much as he does. He knows that he and Lennon share a good friend—rock'n'roll. He can tell that they both listen to the same sounds and, more importantly, hear the same messages. And, most importantly, the music really *matters* to them.

It has been one thing for McCartney to hear the music on the radio or on records, or to see it in the movies or on stage, or even to see local bands that fool around with it. But he can tell that this guy isn't fooling around. This music means something to Lennon—and *he* means business. McCartney holds a sharp eye on this fellow who is in his own age group, in his own city, and playing his own music. It is as if Lennon is incarnating the music for McCartney—rendering the sound waves into something as real as shore waves; taking the notes McCartney hears in each ear and bringing them together into sharp focus behind his eyes, lifting the music off the radio airwaves and putting it into Liverpool air. The deeper mysteries of rock'n'roll begin to crystallize behind McCartney's long, dark brown eyelashes.

As James Paul McCartney sizes up John Winston Lennon near a church on a hill, Lennon's middle namesake, Sir Winston Churchill, is sizing up Britain's role in striving for world peace. Churchill left his post as prime minister in April of 1955. He is speaking at Essex, which is about two hundred miles from Liverpool. Sir Winston rarely appears publicly anymore. But he chooses to make a speech this afternoon on the subject of nuclear armament and testing. He declares:

"In the field of international affairs our achievement in developing unassisted the hydrogen weapon is a helpful contribution. . . .

"I myself believe," proclaims Churchill, "that the weight of evidence lies on the side of those who believe the effects of tests on the present scale to be negligible from the point of view of the health of the human race.

"But even if this were not so," asks Sir Winston, "what are those effects compared with the misery and annihilation of another war? Every addition to the free world's armory increases the chances of permanent peace."

While Churchill gives that speech at Essex, Britain's Secretary of State for Foreign Affairs, Selwyn Lloyd, gives a speech at Liverpool University—but he touches on the subject of nuclear *dis*armament. The university is four-and-a-half miles from the whoop-de-doo in Woolton. Foreign Secretary Lloyd is given an honorary degree of Doctor of Laws at an afternoon ceremony.

After receiving the degree, he says that, as Foreign Secretary, he is trying "to create a world instrument endowed with the necessary authority, not only to keep the peace, but to see that regard is paid to international contracts and obligations."

Lloyd promises "to work for a comprehensive disarmament plan properly controlled so that the world may be free from the threat of war and the burden of armaments, both nuclear and conventional."

Elsewhere in Liverpool, the late afternoon is busy and hot on the cold soup known as the River Mersey. There are ship whistles piping and exports steaming out over churning waters. For those who decide to stay indoors and read the newspaper, the July 6, 1957 *Liverpool Echo* offers today's "Disker's Record Column." Disker is actually Tony Barrow, a journalist who would one day become the press officer for a fairly successful Liverpool rock group. Appearing next to the funnies of Popeye and Blondie and Scamp, the record columnist says that he thinks Elvis Presley is just about finished as a hit-maker. He writes: " 'All Shook Up' is still spinning Mr. Elvis a tidy income in the States but I have an idea the magic has worked for the last time."

The clock on the Victoria Building of the University of Liverpool, on Brownlow Hill, says 4:52 P.M. The sweaty-haired teen named John Lennon brings his band to a close. Applause ripples through the church field. The maverick act is well received. The periodic sun shines summer yellow across Liverpool. With all of Woolton's sun-glittered churches, dozens of crosses stipple dozens of shadows on streets and sidewalks. Then the sun retreats behind clouds again.

As soon as the teenage interlude wraps up, Lennon takes to his heels toward the left side of the stage. He hurries to the scouts' hut on the upper field, going out of his way to avoid his aunt Mimi. He wants to keep himself scarce. In the hut, he huddles with his hand-picked bandmates to talk about their show. They have another one to go at 5:45.

The military band picks up where it left off. Paul McCartney and Ivan Vaughan stroll around and enjoy the Woolton fair of food and fun and females; time for the two teens to play Casanova and look the place over. The field is being set up for the dog show, the day's big attraction.

About twenty minutes later, at 5:11, the military band switches off and the dog show begins. Lennon and his compatriots surface from the scouts' hut to watch. The show is basically an obedience training exhibition. The Liverpool City Police Department puts its German shepherds through their highly disciplined paces. The police are in full uniform, from bobby hats on down. They have the dogs walk across boards, crawl through pipes, jump through hoops.

The exhibition ends at 5:47 and wins the day's biggest patter of hands. Ten minutes pass. The Quarry Men take the stage for their second and final outdoor performance. The sideburned bandleader, John Lennon, looks up at the sea-gray English sky. The sun is a dull bronze. The low clouds are eerie, elfin.

Part III

THE NIGHT
HOURS

EVENING

Like a dexterous pickpocket, a passing cloud steals the sun from the long gray vest of the sky. The cloud edge is black frosted. The shadows on the Liverpool field become more ill defined. It's a summer evening of deepening dampness. The humidity hangs in a dim blue haze. A sudden breeze whispers a warning of whimsical weather.

The Quarry Men Skiffle Group has been on the fairground stage three minutes when the St. Peter's Church belfry peals six o'clock. To the band's lead singer, the chime seems a million light years away. He's deep into his performing. He's also contending with the fact that the pageantry and pace of the fête is winding down like an overwound watch. The carnivalesque mood is atomizing. It has been running down ever since the dog show ended.

The crowd begins to thin out on the kelly green turf. Kids are more caught up in horseplay than fair events.

They've hit all the stalls, tasted all the goodies, ridden all the rides, played all the games. Adults start to wander home for a light dinner. Many will be coming back for the eight o'clock dance at the church hall.

By 6:15 P.M., the pastel air of the field has changed markedly. The perfume of cakes and cookies has dissipated. The pace slackens. The village has spent itself and starts to take a breather. The Quarry Men continue their teenage summer symphony. They keep performing, but it's like performing last rites—doing their job during a dying off. Most of the people who stay around to listen are children and teenagers. One of the teens is the novice guitarist Paul McCartney. The Quarry Men drummer, Colin Hanton, feels hemmed in by the kids who are starting to climb around the stage.

One of Lennon's classmates, Geoff Rhind, jostles his way to the front of the stage. He has a camera in his hand. It's a basic Kodak his parents bought him for his birthday. Rhind raises the camera to his right eye. Lennon is strumming his guitar and spots the camera pointed at him. He sends a willful stare into the little lens. The teenage photographer pushes a button and the shutter winks. A medley of facial features is frozen onto a black-and-white, two-and-a-quarter-inch square negative.

It's 6:32 P.M. when fair organizer Harry Forrest and his crew begin to clear the field. They dismantle stalls, fold up chairs, and start the cleanup. At 6:38, Quarry Men bandleader John Lennon leans into the microphone, draws in a long breath, and thanks the church fête people for having his band today. The teenage musicians gather up their instruments to spirit them across the road for this evening's dance. In the fête program, the event is aggrandized in large dark type: "GRAND DANCE in the CHURCH HALL." Directly below those words is a notice about the night's entertainment: "GEORGE EDWARDS BAND also The Quarry Men Skiffle Group." The George Edwards Band is a dance orchestra that does everything from waltzes to quicksteps.

With a troop-movement nod of his head, Lennon leads his band off the fairgrounds. They carry their equipment, such as it is, along the dirt path next to the church. It's 6:43 P.M. Their gait is brisk as they cross Church Road. The road is a twenty-six-foot, two-inch splinter of a street. The teenage footsteps beat a rock'n'roll tattoo underfoot. The roadway is growing hotter in the July humidity. A batch of sparrows vie for places on roof peaks beneath the lowering clouds.

On the other side of the road is the single-story St. Peter's School and, behind the school, the St. Peter's Church Hall. The teen musicians amble past the school, through a small open courtyard, and up toward the right to the hall's side door.

The St. Peter's Church Hall is a brick building shaped like a steeple-roofed barn. Three long windows, one circular window, and two canopied doors face the small courtyard. The hall is gorged with the ghosts of school plays and village meetings and table-tennis tournaments. There is an auditorium, a kitchen, a stage, an offstage area, and storage rooms.

The auditorium walls are gooped with what the paint cans of the day call "Lakeland Green." The color is more swampish than lake-ish. Eight fat circular bulbs hang from the high ceiling. Wooden and metallic folding chairs outline the thirty-four-by-fifty-six-foot floor area. There's an eleven-tiered set of bleachers in the back of the auditorium. The left back door has a vestibule. Above the vestibule, for the dance tonight, a colored spotlight perches like a sleeping electric peacock. The spinning spotlight will help turn the old hall into Woolton's grand ballroom, the local dance suite of choice.

In the warm evening, the shadowy little church hall is grotto cool. The Quarry Men enter by the side kitchen door. The kitchen gives access to the auditorium. There is the clatter of silverware and plates. A couple of ladies from the church committee smile hello to the teens. The place has the piney smell of Aunt Sally disinfectant. The Quarry Men enter the auditorium and see that the George Edwards Band has already arranged its equipment on the stage. So they put their own not-quite-so-ritzy instruments onstage, in the wings, on chairs. Then the teenagers get down to the serious business of eating and slaking their thirsts. They move about in the deeper shadows, snatching snacks, then pull some folding chairs into a circle near the front of the stage. Holding court is the band's leader, John Lennon. They sit and talk and laugh and eat and drink and smoke. It's a small knot of friends.

At 6:47, less than five minutes after the Quarry Men have arrived at the hall, two more teenagers cross Church Road. It's a humidity ravaged evening as occasional Quarry Man Ivan Vaughan guides his guitarist friend Paul McCartney across the street from the field. McCartney leaves his bike by the side wall and Vaughan shoves open the door. Inside is eternity. They breeze through the kitchen and into the back of the auditorium. McCartney, guitar on his back, looks guardedly toward the stage area where several of the Quarry Men are sitting around laughing. Some of the teenage musicians side-eye the guy in the bright white sports coat. Lennon glances at him cautiously.

As Vaughan leads his friend toward the stage area, McCartney rapidly becomes acclimated to the compact auditorium. The fifteen-year-old hears the church hall habitués talking and laughing and he notices the funny acoustics of the odd shaped building. It's not exactly the Philharmonic on Hope Street, where the young man had been given a first-place prize four years ago, in 1953, for a school essay. The prize had been a book by Geoffrey Trease called *Seven Queens of England*. The teenager notes that the sound of the hall is definitely not fit for a queen—not even a Rose Queen.

Vaughan's face is animated as he prepares to introduce McCartney to the band—and especially to John Lennon. It's a tantalizing prospect to Vaughan: devil-may-care

John meeting cherub-cheeked Paul; the guy who has to practice on the porch meeting the guy who has a piano in the parlor; the class clown who's had a few beers and didn't tell his aunt he had a band meeting the dressed-to-kill kid who is going to scout camp and is encouraged to play music by his father.

McCartney and Vaughan reach the section in front of the stage where the Quarry Men have established their folding-chair sanctum. In the center of the stage, on the back wall, there's a one-foot-square windup clock. It's ten feet above the floor and its Roman numerals indicate 6:48. The saffron light from the oversize church hall windows slings shadows across the teens' faces. The low light accents the angularity of Lennon's nose.

As is usual with teenage guys, the "introductions" are not so much introductions as glances from a poker game on a fast train. None of them are exceedingly concerned with formal niceties. Vaughan tells the people who the guy with him is and then tells the guy with him who the people are, and that's about as ceremonious as it gets. So when McCartney meets Lennon, they don't shake hands —nor do they know that fate is shaking both their hands. In greeting each other, they barely move their lips. Lennon nods faintly, once, involuntarily; McCartney's mouth makes a small smile that does not reach his eyes.

For a millisecond, they eye each other in motionless tableau—Lennon sitting, McCartney standing. Then their eyes meet squarely and, momentarily, you can practically hear the dust motes settle on Lennon's guitar next to him on a chair. The sight each beholds is hardly astonishing:

brown eyes, brown hair, average height, average weight
. . . No, the astonishment would surge from something
inside the two of them—something *behind* the eyes, *under*
the hair, *over* the height, *beyond* the weight; something
about a certain . . . attitude . . . toward a certain . . .
kind . . . of music.

Vaughan and McCartney pull up chairs and join the
group. McCartney takes the guitar off his back and puts it
on a folding chair. There is talk, but none between Lennon
and McCartney. They keep their verbal distance from one
another. They're both casual but not conversational. There's
about as much personal interaction between them as in a
chess game played by mail. The church hall clock puts away
a few minutes and neither Lennon nor McCartney utters
even terse syllables. It's not as if they fumble for words:
they just don't bother talking to each other.

Ivan Vaughan becomes flummoxed by the frostiness between the two teens. Since they're both rock-hard in their
devotion to rocking hard, he had anticipated they would
hit it off. Instead, there are icy walls of detachment. It's
as if they're destined to be like the two Liver Birds on the
Pier Head, facing in opposite directions, never seeing eye
to eye. Vaughan begins to doubt that the two musicians
will ever see eye to eye. He feels as if he has arranged a
meeting on quicksand. One day he will write in his autobiography, "It seems my life was an apprenticeship in
stress and the art of coping."

It is McCartney who ultimately breaks the ice when,
unostentatiously, he stands and picks up his guitar from
the chair next to him and starts to play it. So it is the

guitar that will do the talking between them. It's 6:52 P.M. In the wan light of the church hall, McCartney reaches for the guitar instinctively—like Dickens's Pip reaching for Miss Havisham's tablecloth to put out the fire in her cobwebbed ballroom in *Great Expectations*. He picks up the instrument and feels the thick, acoustic promise of its hollowness and strings. Lennon, still not unthawed, crisscrosses his arms in front of his chest. This dark-haired chap might look a bit like Elvis, thinks Lennon, but he also looks way too young to do anything serious with a guitar.

A few seconds later, Lennon is entranced as McCartney bewitches his guitar into a tuned musical instrument. Destined by his rock'n'roll instincts, the young Elvis semi-look-alike cuts loose on a song by Eddie Cochran called "Twenty Flight Rock." His hands sink into the guitar like a sawblade into wood. His voice and playing and movements are extraordinarily fresh and vibrant. The beat of his music thumps against the hall's marshy green walls. His white jacket flaps around him. The teenager puts his heart and soul and mind on rock'n'roll autopilot, returning the favor of Lennon's show with a show of his own.

When McCartney had started playing, Lennon had been staring moodily at the wall; this improbable guitar player was too young to pay any attention to. The fifteen-year-old has been playing only a matter of seconds when Lennon's eyes cut from the wall to McCartney to the wall . . . and back to McCartney. The light from the big church hall windows seems shrouded, like the light in a dream. To Lennon, the sound floating through the light is a bou-quiet of scented notes. For a second, the sound takes away the very breath that services his brain. His teeth come together suddenly. There is a subdued crunching in his mouth. His skin feels as if it's biodegrading. If eyes could glow, his would be a couple of coast guard searchlights at 4 A.M. He opens his mouth slightly, but no words come out. For once, the Lennon tongue is tied. He stirs in his chair, adjusting his ego. He steeples his fingers together under his chin and leans forward and stares.

McCartney has Lennon's rapt attention. Lennon has a sensation of the hall getting smaller and darker, and McCartney getting bigger and brighter. Lennon feels that touch of gentle giddiness one has on a ship at sea when another ship comes up over the horizon. On rocky Liverpool waves, Lennon and McCartney zigzag into each other's sight.

They *see* each other.

For Lennon, it's not just that the kid knows how to play the guitar. He can tell that McCartney is far more than a mechanic on the instrument. He can tell that McCartney *feels* for the music. He divines that these runaway rock'n'roll sounds travel first class in McCartney's emotional compartment, just as they do with him. Everyone else in that church hall shoves them under a second-class seat. Like McCartney earlier today, Lennon is aware for the first time of someone making rock'n'roll into a Liverpool commodity. Here's a Liverpool kid playing good rock'n'roll, just as he has been trying to do. It's an ineffable realization for Lennon's rock-racked emotions. The air becomes charged with mutual respect. Lennon rests his left ankle on his right knee. As his eyes fill with Mc-Cartney, he becomes aware that he's looking at quite a lot of musician.

Fifteen-year-old Paul McCartney knocks off "Twenty Flight Rock" and gathers more momentum, plunging into Gene Vincent's "Be-Bop-a-Lula." He has no idea that he's opening the book on a friendship that will have all the joy and pain of brotherhood. With a death grip on the guitar, everything in McCartney's being seems concentrated in the ten fingertips of his hands. Dancing fingers lace fast patterns again and again and again up and down the guitar neck; young fingers searching out old truths. Some finely honed phrases emerge from the guitar. The teenager points the instrument ceilingward. The high ceiling gives the room's acoustics a barnlike effect. The nearly empty hall serves as a natural amplifier.

To finish up, McCartney requisitions a medley of Little Richard tunes from his well-stocked musical memory. He sings raucously, unrestrainedly, dropping salvos of strident howls on his young listeners. His voice dives deep into their ear canals. Lennon discerns tonnage in the tonsils. There's the engine of a rock'n'roll rocket in there. The voice paints the church hall ceiling in teen sparkle, whereupon St. Peter's Church Hall, Liverpool, England, becomes rock'n'roll's Sistine Chapel. As he sings, McCartney oscillates rhythmically. Sweat streaks his cheeks and trickles down his neck. He looks at the wheel of faces around him. Above a jacket that is as white and shiny and speckled as a well-exercised cue ball, his glance irradiates darkly.

Lennon listens. He listens and learns. He listens and learns from a Liverpool lad. His eyes riveted on McCartney's fingers, his chin cupped in his hands, his feet stapled to the floor, he sits in silent wonder, squinting. A young man not easily astonished, Lennon is astonished. He has a feeling of seasickness. For his money, McCartney's performance is the teenage apotheosis of rock'n'roll. He contemplates the musical intelligence in the younger fellow's fingers. He gleans the knowledge that McCartney's fingers might know more than his do.

The kid's auspicious exhibition makes Lennon feel the confines of his own musical knowledge. His enjoyment of the show quickly transforms into competitiveness. Agewise, this guy is unimpressive; talentwise, he might just be *too* impressive. Lennon notes how the little show has shushed everyone in the room. McCartney has wrested control of the boys from him and Lennon knows it—there's a new rooster in the church-hall barn. Nonetheless, the older teen cannot ignore the rare sense of admiration McCartney's guitar work has induced in him. Lennon's blood pressure and heartbeat pick up. He's like an astronaut feeling the g-load of liftoff—this g-load being a hot load of rock guitar.

At one point during his Little Richard medley, McCartney has his back to Lennon. The almost-seventeen-year-old wants to keep his eyes peeled on the just-barely-fifteen-year-old's hands—wants to see what his fingers are doing. More than that, he wants to see the kid's face. He wants to read the depth of rock'n'roll there. His poor eyesight is already making it difficult enough for him to see what he wants. Now this dark-haired Elvis-type is facing the other way.

In a trice, the older teen has dropped the tough-guy mask and is leaning unsubtly over the younger teen's white-jacketed shoulder. It's a photo finish as to which rises first: Lennon or his eyebrows. The action is involuntary. He moves in close to the guitarist as naturally as he had moved close to this music in the first place—no psychological fencing about it. If Lennon stood any closer, he would feel the brush of McCartney's eyelashes on his face.

A bright yellow light creeps through the high church hall windows. Squadrons of shadows overrun the auditorium walls and floors. It's 6:58 P.M. when McCartney polishes off his little gem of a performance. There is the salty tang of sweat in his mouth. The show has lasted six minutes. It has been six minutes of sudden power. He stops playing and notices Lennon staring over his shoulder. The two tongues become amiable over the guitar. McCartney's throat is dry. But he shows Lennon how to play "Twenty Flight Rock," displaying his knowledge like a notch on a belt. Quarry Man guitarist Eric Griffiths also assimilates the dissertation.

Then McCartney showers Lennon with more goodies. He offers to write out the lyrics to "Twenty Flight Rock" and "Be-Bop-a-Lula." He transcribes the songs hyperefficiently. Lennon had been fast to form a band; now fast meets fastidious. The pen pirouettes across the paper in a clear, clean script. He could have dashed off a fistful more. Instead, he shows Lennon and Griffiths how to tune their guitars. With apparent magic in his fingers, McCartney divulges the state secret, and tunes. Lennon watches this epic feat, and learns, and feels as if his arteries are turning into tiny streams of crushed ice. He sees his musical horizons broadening by the second.

The last of the chords takes wing on the viscid evening air. McCartney is energized. The brief show has refreshed him. He's glad he got to play for these guys his own age, especially for Lennon. McCartney feels hungry and his lungs desire fresh air. He says he has to get home, straps his guitar on his back, and makes his adieux. He waves a general good-bye and, with his friend Ivan, soft-shoes it toward the door. Lennon watches the white jacket drift cloudlike across the auditorium. In an eyeblink, it's gone.

The powwow between the two teen rockers is over. It's 7:09 P.M. Elapsed time from McCartney's entrance to exit: twenty-one minutes. Nobody would ever have believed how much pow and how much wow would one day come of those twenty-one minutes. The two teenagers hardly know each other's names. But they are far from strangers: they have bled rock'n'roll into each other's wrists.

Some of the Quarry Men go home, and some of them stick around the church grounds. The dance is scheduled to start at eight. One of those who sticks around is the sideburned guitarist, John Lennon. He wants to steer clear of his aunt Mimi today. He also wants to explore the knowledge imparted to him by that young Liverpool rocker. As he practices in the umbrageous church hall, holding the guitar as if it's a wooden life preserver, the sky darkens slowly. Storm clouds meander by like listless gray alley cats. There is a rising wind cutting through the supersaturated air. Around 7:45, the sky issues a couple of rounds of musket fire. The shadowy ceiling rumbles. Forks of lightning wink over the tops of the church field trees. A wind-spun page of newsprint flips through a gutter. The sky continues to blacken.

As advertised, the "GRAND DANCE in the CHURCH HALL" kicks off at 8 P.M. The George Edwards Band is booked to open and close the dance. They will play from 8:00 to 8:45; 9:15 to 10:00; and 10:30 to 11:00—a total of two hours. The Quarry Men Skiffle Group will play two half-hour sets, one from 8:45 to 9:15 and the other from 10:00 to 10:30. The rollicking mood perks up anew at the dance. The two-shilling admission is collected at the back doors. Over the back door with the vestibule, a teen-ager slowly spins the multicolored spotlight, shedding a party flush on the regalement. Kids compete for seats on the bleachers. Teens compete for each other's attention. Adults compete with age to keep on dancing. Church committee ladies walk about the premises with blue-trimmed plates of cakes and tea and orangeade and sausage rolls. The church hall has a family feeling inside.

Outside, across Church Road, the sloping green field is windswept. The sky is the darkest it has been all day. A distant thunderclap rends the day's harmony. Some of the chipperness at the dance turns to startlement. Another detonation fulminates in a menacing clap. That brings a few hard stares from the church hall. The wind starts to bluster. There are a couple of wide, light-blue flashes in the sky. The River Mersey—that holder of Liverpool's memory—seems to be disappearing. A frosty looking white cloud walks across the river with ghost-of-Christmas-future steps. The Dickensian cloud mass reaches Liverpool's piers and enters the city. It meets the people who are out at eight o'clock for a Saturday evening—housewives and husbands, bellhops and beauticians, dockers and rockers, office workers and factory workers, children allowed to stay up late and elderly who don't want to be called "the late." When the 8 P.M. curtain goes up at Liverpool's Royal Court Theatre for a showing of *The Pajama Game*, an American musical, the phantasmic cloud is fingering the theater's front door.

In America at eight o'clock, Evangelist Billy Graham takes the stage at New York's Madison Square Garden to expostulate on "What Is Faith?" Although it's the Saturday of a July Fourth Independence Day weekend, seventeen thousand people turn out to see Graham. His presentation is televised live from 8 to 9 P.M. on Channel 7. At 8:30 tonight, Louis Armstrong plays a "Jazz Jamboree" at City College of New York. The better seats are $1.20. All others are 50¢. Entertainment this evening at New York's Paramount Theater on Broadway and 43rd Street is billed as "Alan Freed and his Rock'n'Roll Stage Show." For Americans spending the holiday weekend at home instead of going fishing, the TV catch of the evening is *The Lawrence Welk Show* at 9 P.M. on Channel 7. The featured performer tonight is named Rockwell.

Forty-five minutes into the upcountry dance in Liverpool, England, it's time for the teen band called the Quarry Men to rock well. The group's lead singer-guitarist has played on this three-foot-high church hall stage before. He has gotten up there to play his guitar, informally, at Saturday night Youth Club dances. Tonight he starts his band off with the youth segment of the audience in mind. The Quarry Men have been playing for about one hot minute when the day finally blows a fuse. A cold blue finger of lightning points crookedly at the Liverpool landscape. The storm takes over the sky. The air crackles with thunderboomers. There is a sudden driving rain. The storm's starting time: 8:46—less than two hours since a couple of pent-up rock'n'roll fanatics shared glances and a guitar lesson.

A choppy wind slants the rain hard against the hall's peaked roof. The church field hisses under the downpour. The rain plasters the grass to the earth. The sky rumbles with falling bowling pins. Lightning flashes of purple-blue are applauded by thunderclaps. Since Liverpool rarely has thunderstorms, the people aren't at all accustomed to this kind of onslaught out of the blue. Some are startled, even alarmed, by the thunder rolls and the raincloak and the flashes. Their alarm magnifies when the storm knocks out the church hall lights for a few minutes.

All Liverpool is washed by the strong, cool, spindrift rain. The thundershower spatters the city like a glass of beer thrown into a frying pan. The wind spoons big feathery whitecaps across the Mersey River. Instead of flowing in a current, the Mersey swirls.

The storm tears savagely at people and places. Anyone out for a Saturday night on the town is running for shelter. Most are soaked to the skin before they find it. The petals of bright red roses tremble in the high wind. There is a steady beat of slamming windowpanes. Prince Albert, sitting on a horse in front of St. George's Hall, holds his hat in his right hand. Across the street, a tired-looking, white-haired fellow wishes he had that hat. He finds a dry haven in a red wood and glass public call box, or phone booth.

Telephone lines go down in various parts of northern England. There are also blackouts and beached boats. In Nottingham, a cricket match between Britain and the West Indies is halted. The hard winds fly in the face of the two Liver Birds at the top of the Pier Head. Elsewhere in Liverpool, lightning strikes a chimney at St. John Bagot Hospital on Netherfield Road. No one is hurt.

The rain and wind start to abate shortly after nine o'clock. The storm finally calls it quits at 9:20. The hot day is broken. A light breeze blows across the city.

The air is clear and fresh and ready for new life.

SUNSET

Paul McCartney and his younger brother Mike catfoot around the second floor of their home at 20 Forthlin Road. A piquant pipe smell laced with lavender permeates the house. For the older brother, the events of a couple of hours ago in the St. Peter's Church Hall have already turned into yesterday. Asserting his talents is not the most pressing matter to him tonight.

The most pressing matter is preparing a surprise for his father's birthday tomorrow. Born July 7, 1902, Jim McCartney will be fifty-five. Lately, the teenage Paul has often thought about the subject of his father's age. Maybe fifty-five isn't, say, sixty-four, but it is still getting on some and deserves notice. So while the Liverpool sky goes crash and boom tonight, the two McCartney brothers don't pay any heed. They're too busy trying to cook up a nice birthday surprise. It's just a felicitous summer evening at home for them; unthunderstruck, as it were. They decide to go downstairs and see if they can come up with any ideas. They had bought him a Havana cigar at Christmas, so it's going to take some thinking to top that.

Soon-to-be-fifty-five Jim McCartney is lounging in his favorite easy chair in the parlor. His left ankle is crossed over just above his right knee. He has solemn eyes and slicked-back hair. His sons and his piano and his hand-sewn tobacco pouches and his gardening provide him his pleasures; his arthritis provides him his pain. This evening he sits with his slippers on and puffs on his pipe. He's situated in the chair so that his left ear is toward the room. He damaged his right eardrum at age ten.

His two sons come down the stairs. Mike goes into the pantry for jam butties. Paul steps into the front parlor and sits down. His father is smoking his pipe and doing "Your Daily Cross-Word" in today's *Liverpool Echo*. The newspaper sits propped up on his left knee. Jim McCartney is an old warrior at crisscrossing crossword battlefields. He does the puzzle almost every day. Sometimes his boys do it with him. There's a dog-eared dictionary next to his chair and he has the boys look up words when they work the puzzle. Tonight the pencil pauses over the lower right-hand corner of page two . . . Let's see: *1 across*—a six-letter word for "seek." The elder McCartney pencils in S-E-A-R-C-H . . . *27 down*—a five-letter word for "record." Jim McCartney pencils in E-N-T-E-R.

His son Paul sits across the room and tries to enter the father's mind: what could they do for him as a surprise for his birthday? The pencil dances across the newspaper. His father whistles lightly. Smoke from the pipe climbs a corkscrew staircase to the ceiling and hangs flat, like a veil. The ashtray is lined with lavender from the back garden. The teenager looks at the newspaper on his father's lap and remembers him looking at the horseracing results earlier. Young Paul wishes he were rich—then he'd *buy* the man a horse, a powerful steed that would win at Aintree. As it is, the only horse they have around is the clotheshorse that holds the weekly ironing.

His brother Mike enters the room with the sandwiches. Jim McCartney looks up. Then the father's eyes wander over to his older son. He's not happy about how Paul is wearing his hair and dressing lately. And he's not positive that this labyrinthine absorption in the guitar is all for the good. But he's a teenager; he's growing up. Jim McCartney puffs on his pipe and takes careful note of his son. He ponders how the little boy he used to hoist over his head and onto his shoulders for piggyback rides is not such a little boy anymore. Nowadays he's even too big to sit on his father's knee while the once-upon-a-time maestro of Jim Mac's Jazz Band plays the piano. The father finds himself wanting to go with the boy when he buys his trousers so he doesn't have the legs narrowed so tightly, in the style of the day. As the father tinkers with the riddle known as adolescence, he's not sure whether he's witnessing a sunrise or a sunset.

Before the sun sets on the Liverpool daytide of July 6, 1957, there is a delicate summer twilight. It's 9:24 P.M. and a potent freshness injects the air. The sun comes out weakly. It flicks tiny flecks of gold on Woolton Village.

But the sun is an old candle that has been guttered once too often this day. In the gloaming, a stately elm bows its water-logged branches. The cemetery next to St. Peter's Church has become a muddy quagmire. Rivulets of rain run across the grave of Eleanor Rigby.

Directly across the street from her grave, facing her gravestone in fact, the St. Peter's Church Hall dances the night away. The Quarry Men have just finished their first half-hour set about ten minutes ago. The band cooked up its usual blend of rock and skiffle tunes and they had the teens twitching. Lennon's throat feels faintly constricted. Now the George Edwards Band is on and the teen light-heartedness is infectious. The farmer and the quarry man and the teacher solidify in neighborly kinship. The organizers of the fête attract praise from all quarters. Some of the fête workers look bedraggled. The principal organizer, Harry Forrest, has the strange sensation of being anxiety free. He's ready to doze off into a deep oblivion.

By 9:40 P.M. the Liverpool sun is a disappearing disk. It has worked a long, erratic day. After all the booming from above, it's a quiet summer sundown. The westering sun gives the River Mersey a coppery afterglow. The evenfall shuts Liverpool down like the red lid of a box. For a few moments, the horizon is rose-colored ground glass. The city is tiring with the onset of dusk. A railway clerk yawns as a three-cylinder locomotive percolates plumes of steam into the no longer steamy air. Parlor pianos fill the soft summer night with soft summer songs. A speeding fire engine screams down Madryn Street, blue light aswirl. By popular demand, the New Brighton Bathing Pool will stay open tonight for "floodlit bathing" until eleven o'clock. In Penny Lane, a slow-chewing old man waits for a bus under the glint-shot sky. His eyes keep hurrying along his watch chain to his watch.

The public houses do a good business this hour. They're getting ready to close at ten o'clock. Whether in the White Horse or the Elephant or the Grapes, relaxed hands clasp wide pint tumblers. In some tumblers, it's "a pint of bitter," in others, "a pint of mild." At Johnson's Appliances, on 10 Woolton Street, the premier item on sale tonight is the television set. The owners bill themselves as "Pioneers of Television in Liverpool." They even offer "Evening TV Demonstrations every Thursday night from 7:30 to 10." Most of the TVs have seventeen-inch screens and long, outsize black backs. The average price of a television set at Johnson's is 89 pounds ($249.20). Still on call on Woolton Street tonight are the doctors at the medical office of Warner, McCullagh, and Burrows. They're family doctors who will make house calls any time of the day or night. Even if you move, your family doctor will usually stay with you.

While the Woolton doctors do their doctoring and the St. Peter's fête revelers do their reveling, there is another Liverpool fête capping off its day. This afternoon the Mossley Hill Parish Church also had its big event. The high point of their fête was a performance by the men's Morris Dancers. The group has been around for twenty years. A reporter from the *Liverpool Weekly News* asks if the group can dance rock'n'roll. Secretary-treasurer Ernest Winter replies, "We think it is rather a dull way of spending an evening. We, of course, can do rock'n'roll. But what's the point?"

Many of those who don't attend fête dances tonight in Liverpool are taking in a movie. Rolling since 9:20 P.M. at the Liverpool Odeon is *The Steel Bayonet*. A Gary Cooper movie called *Friendly Persuasion* is playing at the Empire Garston. Grace Kelly, Bing Crosby, and Frank Sinatra star in *High Society* at the Mayfair. *The River's Edge*, with Ray Milland, is playing at the Abbey Theatre.

As well as all the fun of the movies and shopping and drinking and swimming and dancing this Saturday evening, there will also be death in Liverpool. In a tragic auto accident, a Liverpool woman named Mary McGreal is knocked down and killed by a car just after ten o'clock. A resident of Huntley Road, she had been crossing at the corner of Prescot Road and Hinton Street. In another Saturday evening tragedy, a Liverpool ship loses a British seaman in the Sea of Japan. The ship is forty miles from land when eighteen-year-old Arlon Roberts falls overboard. The 5,818-ton freighter, *Ramon de Larrinaga*, is owned by a Liverpool steamship company. The crew spends the night searching dark waters for the seaman.

In the United States this year, many car drivers are, for the first time, choosing smaller automobiles. The most popular small car of 1957, selling 200,000 this year, is put out by Volkswagen. It's called the Beetle. The U.S. State Department publishes a volume today about international events in 1940, the last year of America's World War II neutrality. The 916-page document includes several messages to then-president Franklin D. Roosevelt from Winston Churchill, who used the code name, "former naval person." And on this day of a rare thunderstorm over Liverpool, Dr. Herbert L. Jones, a weather expert at Oklahoma A & M College, releases new findings that classify five types of lightning.

Just as arbitrary fate would deal death cards in England today, so there would be tragedy an ocean away in the United States. This evening, in Florida, four Navy crewmen are killed when their A3D Douglas twinjet bomber explodes in midair and crashes. The bomber falls in a wooded site between a Boy Scout camp and a residential area near Sanford. The crew had been practicing landings. In Westhampton, New York, thirty-two-year-old Robert A. Cuddihy is driving his convertible along Dune Road at night when he hits a utility pole. The heir to the Funk and Wagnalls publishing fortune, Cuddihy is thrown from the car and dies hours later. On Lake Ontario, three men from Rochester, New York, are tossed into the water when their small boat overturns. One of them survives by clinging to the capsized boat for over eight hours. His name is John Speciale.

A special day is culminating at this hour in Liverpool, England. The clock dial in front of the Midland Bank in Penny Lane reads 10:45. At the Woolton church hall dance, the Quarry Men have done their second half-hour set and the George Edwards Band is putting on the finishing touches. Woolton is partied out. The people are tired. There's more talking than dancing at this point. The fête is ready to fold its tent for another year. The lights in the church hall will be snapped off at eleven.

Some people leave early. They exit the hall and notice that the air has cooled. A rain-soaked flag droops next to St. Peter's School. There are puddles at the curbs. When the people arrive home, some of them take a quick look at their nightly newspaper, the *Liverpool Evening Express*. Its front-page headline tonight reads:

MERSEYSIDE SIZZLES

PHEW!
AGAIN
TODAY

The story starts off: "All Merseyside sizzled in another scorcher today . . ."

On page four of the paper there is an article by a professional journalist about the music business. The article says: "It always shocks me to find that an unknown singer can be shot into the big-money class on the variety stage these days on the mere strength of one gramophone record. Yet it keeps happening."

The writer's name is George Harrison.

NIGHT

Night falls and the rinsed windows of Liverpool glow in soft diffused yellows. Slate rooftops glisten with the night's rain. The Mersey River is black volcanic glass edged in moonglow. A middle-aged fellow with time-beaten eyes and a swarthy walrus mustache stands on a wharf and stares out over the water. He watches a small ship belching gray smoke. The ship sluices a bridal train of foam in its wake.

It has been a dizzying day of changing weathers—but doggedly hot. Brimstone is on the loose. Throughout most of July 6, 1957, the sun has been a big yellow boil on the back of Western Europe. This tenth consecutive day under the heat wave's yoke has been tortuous. In Rheims, France, the temperature hit 98 degrees. In Paris, it was 97. In Bonn, West Germany, police have to tussle with an epidemic of bike-stealing. People are so hot, they just don't want to walk anymore—and so conscience is flung to the steamy wind. The heat twists its grasping fingers around other parts of the world as well. Mexico City, for example, has a high temperature of 126 degrees. Thirty-eight persons die heat-related deaths there today.

In Woolton, Liverpool, an innocuous breeze draws a sigh from the leafy branches bordering the church field. The leaves on the trees behind the absent wooden stage nod quietly. The spacious church grounds are empty. The gold clock in the weathered sandstone church chimes 11 P.M. The St. Peter's Church tower looks sullenly over the moon-streaked field. The phase of the moon is just past first quarter. The sun silvers a little over half the oval that faces the earth. Leave shapes cover the field in crow-footed shadows. The last happy voice has died away on the fairground. The afternoon's gaiety is now history. Prosaic life has invaded the empty grassland. The annual grand fling is over.

With nightfall, the squally day is ready to be filed and forgotten. By eleven o'clock, the stalls and folding chairs from the fête have been stacked away in the church hall. When all is reckoned, the day raises close to 1,000 pounds for St. Peter's Church. Now, as the church hall doors are locked, the main consideration on most people's minds is getting home and grabbing some sacktime. The village will be abed by midnight.

As teenage bandleader John Lennon breaks camp in the church hall, he has a used-up mien. He looks like a fifty-year-old man after an all-night pub crawl. There is a hot, rasping feeling in the back of his throat. His mood has seesawed all day. He feels like a clock that needs winding. He feels spent . . . but it is the happy, affordable spent of the young. He's happy mostly because he has im-bibed—even *publicly* imbibed—his spiritual nutrition for the day. He has played rock'n'roll.

Some of his performance tonight was even recorded. Teenager Bob Molyneux is an audiotaping hobbyist, Len-non acquaintance, and member of the church Youth Club. This evening he stood in front of the stage and held up the microphone of his portable Grundig TK8. Molyneux caught about ten songs on Phillips three-inch reel-to-reel tapes, including Lonnie Donegan's "Puttin' on the Style" and Elvis Presley's "Baby, Let's Play House."

Lennon departs from the church hall with his temples throbbing. He has something on his mind. The quick brain is racing. What's haunting him is the afterimage of the dark-haired teenager in the white jacket. He still can't get over the kid—or his rock'n'roll. It has been a long day of music for the sixteen-year-old. But it's never too late in the day for him to think about rock'n'roll. He senses there is much fine music in this McCartney fellow —young as he looks. He conceives of McCartney's musical self as a lion in a cage that's not nearly strong enough to hold it.

Whether Lennon likes it or not, he knows that the two of them are bookends: there are volumes of rock'n'roll feel-ings between them. That had been something he felt in his bones before McCartney had even been playing a full minute. Already sure that Elvis is his rock'n'roll father, he muses over whether he has now met his rock'n'roll brother, his first rock'n'roll brother.

The problem sliding through the grooves of Lennon's brain is what to do next. He has thoughts of asking Mc-Cartney to join his band. In playing musical ping-pong with McCartney, the band would get better and his own guitar playing would mature. Lennon feels he has a mandate to improve both his band and himself. Also, given McCartney's choice of tunes today, he can tell he'd have a partner in steering the band toward rock'n'roll, away from skiffle.

But the prospect of asking McCartney to join the group hammers Lennon's ego against the anvil of his ambitions. True, he wants a rock'n'roll band. Absolutely, he wants the best band possible. He wants someone to fan the flame of his own inchoate talent. Yet, if McCartney turns out to be better than he is, Lennon might end up playing second fiddle. And if there's any instrument he knows he'll never learn, that's the one. Musically, he will be at no one's beck and call. Nor does he want to lose the leadership of his band and see the group go off in a different direction.

Still, when all is said and done, the compass needle of Lennon's feelings points toward McCartney. The guy *sounds* right. The guy *looks* right. The guy *knows* his rock'n'roll. The guy seems *young* enough not to threaten his management. The idea *feels* right. And that about clinches it for him, since Lennon puts what he feels over what he thinks. He decides to compare notes with his best friend, Pete

Shotton, as they walk home tonight. They're the guardian sentries to the front door of the Quarry Men.

The two teenagers cross Church Road. They sniff the rain-cleared air. There's the strong scent of a wet, freshly cut lawn. The nocturnal strollers walk by St. Peter's Church. In front of the church, close to the sidewalk, is a tall, oblong war memorial. It's dated 11 November, 1918. Besides that date, the only other inscription chiseled into the sandstone is at eye level so that people will see it each day. Two feet wide by seven inches deep, it's a single, capitalized word: PEACE. John Lennon, guitar in his right hand, and Pete Shotton, under his yellow mass of curly hair, walk past the memorial. Lennon carries the guitar lightly like a fishing rod, not heavily like a rifle. Late as it is, the guitarist's step is light. Even the guitar in his hand feels light. Of far more weight is the memory he carries of the teenager who played "Twenty Flight Rock" in the church hall this evening, a hundred years ago.

The two friends tread the Woolton sidewalks, and Lennon dishes out his usual doses of arsenic wit. Even in the boneyard of night, he could make light of everything. They duck the wet, overhanging leaves. Pools of water sparkle in the cobbled gutters. The curb-parked, oily looking puddles are as shiny and dark as a fleet of brand-new limousines. Never one for foot-dragging, Lennon asks Shotton what he would think about having McCartney in their band. Shotton turns his eyes toward his sideburned friend. Lennon stares vacantly at the twig-peppered sidewalk in front of him. Shotton can tell it's no blarney. They talk it over and he tells Lennon he has no problem with the idea. Lennon nods.

They want to clear their heads, so they're taking the long way home. They rove down Beaconsfield Road and pass the arboreous grounds of Strawberry Field. Beads of rain shimmer on the tree leaves. Lennon glances at the tall, curlicued iron gates. They remind him of the gates at the front of Graceland, the hundred-thousand-dollar home that Elvis Presley bought in March. Lennon had seen a picture of the thirteen acre Tennessee estate in a magazine. He thinks about the rumors that Elvis will tour England this summer. Then he considers whether Strawberry Field is his own Graceland. So far as he's concerned, it's graceful enough.

The young men turn left onto Menlove Avenue. They reach Shotton's street, Vale Road, and Lennon bids him good-bye. The teen guitarist arrives at the less graceful, much smaller front gates of 251 Menlove Avenue. He turns and walks toward the front door.

In the United States, three New York men in their early twenties are arrested for the theft of a carton of seventeen .22-caliber automatic pistols. In the New York area, a Tyrone Power film is being televised on Channel 11. It started at 10 P.M. and is called *Thin Ice*.

In Grand Central Station, New York City, a twelve-man rigging crew is making final preparations for an atomic missile to go on display tomorrow morning. A sixty-three foot Supersonic Redstone ballistic missile will greet commuters at the east end of Grand Central's upper level concourse. Sleek tail fins glitter across the terminal from the medium-range ground-to-ground missile. The rigging crew is rushing tonight to get the missile perfectly centered on its launching platform for Sunday morning's scheduled showing.

U.S. Vice President Richard M. Nixon is enjoying the denouement of a relaxing day off. The vice president has spent his Saturday in Ontario, Canada, swimming, fishing, boating—a day away from work, a day of peace. In Mount Vernon, Ohio, seven letters by American author Nathaniel Hawthorne are found in a safe deposit box. The dates of the letters range from 1821 to 1858. Hawthorne served as American consul in Liverpool from 1853 to 1857. Of Americans born on July 6, the day belongs to John Paul Jones, a naval hero, and Bill Haley, a teenage hero. Born in 1925, Haley is the first rock'n'roll star.

In Liverpool, England, there is another rock'n'roll birthday, but nobody knows it yet. Nobody knows that a band has been born today. A teenager named John has met a teenager named Paul at a church social, and a rock'n'roll group will come of them. It's only a matter of time, merciless time. The Pier Head clock facing the River Mersey continues its inexorable reckoning. The face of the clock has watched impassively over the two teens since the days they were born. It has seen the two boys at home, in school, on the street. It has seen them in various stages of laughter and tears, warmth and chill, play and sleep. It has seen them on Christmas Days, summer days, birthdays. It has seen John's father leave and Paul's mother die, and it has seen many of their ancestors come and go. Today, for the first time, it has seen the two boys see each other. It has seen them draw breaths from the same air: two musically pure, romantic spirits, unflawed by time or fatigue or limits. The glowing Liverpool clock fights the night like a giant table lamp in a black galactic parlor.

Sixteen-year-old John Lennon opens the front door of Mendips and enters the hallway. Down at the end of the hallway there's a watercolor of a Chinese vase. It was painted by his late uncle George. Lennon doesn't notice it. He's too busy trying to avoid running into his aunt. He swaps greetings with his dog, Sally, and promises to take her out in a few minutes. He has seen enough dog-walking for a while. The teenager doesn't detect the cats around, so he assumes they've all been blessed with sleep. He goes up the stairs. With each step, he feels the day slide slowly off him. His teen-timed footfalls do not echo on the small staircase.

There's a landing light on outside his room. Lennon enters the boxlike room, flicks on his lamp, and puts his guitar down. He closes the door and clicks the lamp off. He drops his lean young body on the bed and twines his hands behind his head. He wants a few minutes to think. Then he'll take the dog out and get ready for bed. He steps into himself. He wishes he had a smoke. The submarine vision of his inner world sinks to periscope depth. Time begins to disappear. His face becomes a clock with no hands. He goes beyond time. A little lake of yellow streams under the door from the light on the landing. At Liverpool Airport, there is the whine of a light aircraft taking off.

Lennon ponders again whether he should ask that Elvis-looking guy to join the band. Left to his own thoughts now, he knows he should ask him. That's all there is to it. There will be no more temporizing about it. If he were another kind of young man, less complicated, he might climb out his bedroom window right now to meet up with this guy Paul—a 1950s Tom climbing out his bedroom window to meet Huck. But a British version of *Tom Sawyer*, Chapter 9, the night isn't to be. The river nearby is the Mersey, not the Merseysippi. Plus the fact that Lennon would sooner go outside in baggy pants and a crewcut than come on as anxious about anything.

He looks at the darkened Elvis Presley poster in his room. A bright smile begins to play across his face. The smile grows into one of Lennon's sleepy-cat grins. He starts to silently mouth the words to Elvis's "Hound Dog." If Elvis is the hound dog, thinks Lennon, then *he'll* be the fox in the big green English field—and give Elvis a run for his money.

The tousle-haired teenager closes his lion-brown eyes and wonders what it would be like to be rich and famous for playing rock'n'roll all day.

He can just Imagine.

It would be a night of a thousand unseen stars shining on in the darkness.

AFTERWORD

The mighty Beatles of yore finished their career as a band on a summery Friday in London when they crossed Abbey Road (for their last album cover), but they *started* it on a summery Saturday in Liverpool by crossing *Church* Road.

I have tried to render a close-up portrait of the day of that first crossing. In 1986, I began seeking out and digging up information about July 6, 1957. Two years later, I did my first round of interviews in England. Then I intensified the research to reconstruct the city of Liverpool as it was in the late fifties. I also broadened the canvas by searching out what was going on that day in other parts of the world. Before I knew it, it was eight years later, and I'd read for hundreds of hours, conducted dozens of interviews, traveled thousands of miles, and spent one long month at the typewriter.

To start the research, I read (or in many cases, reread) books about the Beatles, about Liverpool, about 1957; and about the wide variety of people and events that furnish the real-life backdrop of the book's setting. I also pored over works of literature which involve Liverpool or in some way deepened my understanding of what I was writing about. In addition to books, I took note of many magazines and newspapers.

Besides reading, I looked at many photos and movies and videos germane to this book's characters, time period, and setting. I also listened to, and conducted, many recorded interviews on the subject of that July day.

More useful, however, than ransacking books and movies and tapes was going to Liverpool, itself. The image I always had of the Beatles' Liverpool was of a rough, tough city of tenement slums and industrial soot. Then I went there and saw that the image was wrong. I went looking for a lump of coal; I found a blade of grass. I felt a little like Norman Rockwell felt when researching his illustrations for Mark Twain's *Tom Sawyer* and *Huckleberry Finn*. He took the trouble to visit Twain's hometown of Hannibal, Missouri—the first illustrator to do so. What he found was that the actual details of the town differed from those in the pictures that artists had been drawing for years.

Naturally, I took in all the picture book stops such as Strawberry Field and Penny Lane. But I also left the lanes and the fields to find the paths and the alleys. I wanted to get an authentic feeling for the area, so I delved into places that the tour buses pass by. I recall, in particular, trekking down a long, narrow, shadowy path to look across the quarry behind St. Peter's Church. The tiny path was so midge-ridden, I had to walk with my trenchcoat over my head.

Along with the big-name Beatle spots and the little out-of-the-way places, I put some legwork into experiencing the tremendous scope of physical Liverpool. One day I was so absorbed in the streets and buildings that I came within inches of physically *joining* the landscape. Not used to vehicles driving on the "wrong" side of the road, I started to cross a busy street, checking traffic to my left. A woman put her open hand on my arm and stopped me as a double-decker bus sped by from the right. She thereby saved the Liverpool Police Department the trouble of ruining a good paint scraper while prying my remains off the roadway.

Looking the wrong way while crossing streets wasn't the only habit of mine that died hard in Liverpool. I found myself spending a good deal of time haunting the city's libraries. I was trying to comprehend everything I could about the historical, geographical, cultural, architectural, psychological, musical, political, artistic and social factors that forged Lennon and McCartney's extraordinary creative alliance. So I sat at quaint old desks looking at books and newspaper clippings and microfilm. It was at those desks that I found the little slivers of detail that brought to life the sites I was seeing and the history I had been reading. The word *Liverpool* and the year *1957* began to meld and to come alive in shape and smell and color and movement.

Yet, more revealing than any book or place or clipping I came across in my research was interviewing and getting to know Liverpool's people. Both Lennon and McCartney have given their versions of their first meeting to various interviewers over the years, sometimes contradicting even themselves. To see the day more clearly, I tried to track down people who had been associated with the fête. I looked for the people who organized it, played music at it, operated stalls, decorated the stage, etc. I came up lucky, talking to dozens of people. They ranged from the fellow in charge of running the '57 fête, to most of John Lennon's band, to a guy who happened to snap a picture of John playing that day. Watching my audio tapes turn silently, I became as interested in *who* these Liverpool people were as in *what* they were saying. Their characters, in other words, told me as much about Liverpool as their stories.

As for *Beatle* stories, specifically, the people of Liverpool clearly have a feeling of family toward the group's music and memory. When they talk about one of them, it's often as if they're talking about a son or brother, depending on the speaker's age. To make a rock'n'roll analogy, it's the way Roger Daltrey talked about the late Freddie Mercury at the Mercury tribute concert in 1992 at London's Wembley Stadium. In a backstage interview after the show, I asked Daltrey to characterize Mercury's life work. Just as the people of Liverpool understand life in their hometown, Daltrey understands lead-singing and losing a bandmate. So, in describing Mercury as a "virtuoso," his voice was laden with emotion, as if he were talking about a brother. That's the sense you get from many of the Liverpool people who lived through the Beatles' heyday.

But even as the smiling English faces talked with their

eyes glued to the rear view mirror, I saw a familiar bump in the road ahead. That bump had to do with the fact that memory often plays an extremely complicated riff. People's memories, that is to say, sometimes contradict one another. And in this case the contradictions were on points both small and large.

I wasn't surprised. I had already run across many contradictions about July 6, 1957, in my pre-interview research. From the actual date that John met Paul to where they met to who did what next, there have been several versions. And that's natural. People can't agree on exactly what they saw *seconds* after it happened. So they can't be expected to agree on everything *decades* after it happened. In fact, as the surviving Beatles did interviews in early 1994 for their "official" history, it was Paul McCartney who pointed out that they didn't agree all the time on how things had happened.

I accepted, at the outset of this project, that the best I could do would be to approximate the events of the day. People ask for the "final, authoritative, official, absolutely-without-a-doubt, factual, this-is-how-it-really-was" story of public figures. But you can't get exactly what happened on points that can't be documented by evidence. On those points, you have to rely on interviews. And people will sometimes disagree—those quirky memory riffs will start running into one another.

When I reached forks in the trail of information, I took a careful, unbiased approach. My criteria for reconstructing the reality of July 6, 1957, were, first of all, physical evidence and, barring that, either the preponderance of corroboration among sources, or the logic of the information in relation to established facts. For example, John Lennon once told an interviewer that he was so certain of the date he met Paul McCartney that he had written it down: "June 15, 1955." The Beatles' "authorized" biography gives this date: "June 15, 1956." But it was the actual program of the Woolton church fête that clinched it with this date on the cover: "6th July, 1957." Beatle author Mark Lewisohn was, as usual, correct.

In an introduction to one of John Lennon's books, Paul McCartney said that he and John were twelve years old on the day they met. But birth certificates indicate that John was sixteen, almost seventeen, and Paul had just turned fifteen. Lennon's half-sister, Julia Baird, says in her book that she was at the "St. Paul's Parish Fête," but that John's Aunt Mimi was *not* there. Meanwhile, John's aunt had very specific memories of being at the fête—which was sponsored by St. *Peter's* Church, not St. Paul's. One other thing she remembered with certainty was the unvaryingly sunny weather that day. According to records at Liverpool Airport, there were plenty of clouds.

As I point out these discrepancies, I do so in the full knowledge that this book *also* does not tell the exact story of what happened that day in England. My main goal was not to preside over a collection of Beatle minutiae but, rather, to make manifest the *spirit* of July 6, 1957, Liverpool; to get at the sense of what it was like to be alive at that time, in that place. While I have made the book as factually accurate as possible, I've tried just as hard to extract from those facts the essence of the day—to transmute the dusty facts into living images.

Above all, what I hope I've brought to the Beatle book party is the interplay of teenagers John Lennon and Paul McCartney with the whole process of living Liverpool. Because Beatle music goes straight to the heart in a way that no other music can, I wanted this to be a *people* book, not a *superstar* book. For if Elvis was the *Iliad* of American popular culture, unearthing and embodying a racial and generational war, then the Beatles were the *Odyssey*, chronicling and defining the daily war of coming home to personal truth.

In attempting this transmutation of superstar facts into people images, I've made much of how John and Paul felt about seeing each other play for the first time. Rock'n'roll meant the world to them both, but until that July day in the late fifties, neither had met anybody else who felt the same way. Seeing this hot new American music emanate from teenage Liverpool hands must have hit them where they lived. Yet neither John nor Paul was known to wear his heart on his sleeve. One of McCartney's teachers, for example, recalls the young man returning to school after the biggest tragedy in his life, his mother's death in 1956, and seeming okay—just a bit more reserved. He knew how to publicly contain even his deepest feelings, as did Lennon.

Just because the two teens didn't display or articulate strong feelings at their first meeting doesn't mean they didn't *have* them. I know that many writers don't see the day that way. Most, in fact, downplay the day's events. One McCartney biography goes so far as to say, "There were no bolts of lightning that day." Yet, given how important rock music was to both teenagers, I can't picture either of them not being stirred at the sight of the other performing. Sparks *had* to fly in their rock'n'roll hearts. The simple fact is that for many years following, they chose each other above all others.

In essence, there really *were* bolts of lightning that day—and not just figuratively. During the course of my research, I had tracked down the exact times John Lennon's band, the Quarry Men, had performed on that simmering summer Saturday. I discovered that, according to weather bureau records, one of the performances coincided with the arrival of a thunderstorm. Then, when I was interviewing Bob Molyneux, the fellow who taped the Quarry Men playing that evening, he offhandedly mentioned that the lights had gone out during one song. I asked him why. He said there had been a bad thunderstorm. To have such a subtle point of research so casually confirmed was reassuring, if a little spooky. It made the day come even more alive for me. Apparently, I was getting some of the story right.

If I'm going to lay claim to any sort of accuracy, then an area that requires some explanation is my reporting on international events. The book describes several non-Liverpool, non-British events as taking place on July 6, 1957. They include events of sports, science, music, politics, etc. Initially, I had tried to work these events exactly into the time frame of the book, which is British Summer

Time. For example, if an event took place in New York at noon, I would place it in the time slot of 5 P.M. in the book, since English time is five hours ahead of U.S. Eastern time.

In so doing, however, I found myself including events that—because of the time differences—occurred on July 5 or July 7 in their own time zones. My solution was to defer to the concept of the day called "July 6, 1957" as it unfolded around the world. An event, for example, that took place at 8 P.M., July 6, 1957, Japanese time, was noted in the text as taking place at 8 P.M., regardless of what time it was in relation to British Summer Time.

So when any international event was written up in the text as having occurred at a given time, that was the time it took place in its own country. If no time was given, then it could have taken place at any time of the day— but definitely on July 6, 1957. By this means, the only events given as being part of the concurrent history of the day were the events of that date.

"That date"—I have, for so long, made my own time stand still on "that date"—just a single day in a single month in a single year—that a friend asked me recently if it had been worth it. All I could think to say was that I had never thought to ask myself the question . . . so I guess it *had* been worth it. Now, as I finally let go of this manuscript, I realize just how "worth it" this project has been to me.

Since I conceived this as a rock'n'roll book, I'll put my feelings in rock'n'roll terms. I suppose, like most people, I tend to believe I've seen a few things. I saw Bob Dylan race through a 1974 concert as if he'd just remembered he left the water running in the tub. I saw Jefferson Airplane, not in 1967 but in 1970, and not in San Francisco with flowers in my hair, but in Asbury Park, New Jersey, with sand in my swimming trunks. I saw Led Zeppelin play "Kashmir" at Madison Square Garden just before the *Physical Graffiti* album was released, and so I had no idea about the words Robert Plant was singing (still don't, now that I think about it). I saw Jim Morrison do a concert *cheerily*. I saw Jimi Hendrix yawn.

Having seen all of that, and written a few newspaper columns and a couple of books on rock, I thought I had an idea about what made the heart of rock'n'roll tick. Then I stepped into the St. Peter's Church Hall in Liverpool, England, where John Lennon and Paul McCartney first met, and I felt as if I hadn't seen a thing. I was a rock'n'roll innocent and was, at that moment, hearing the beat for the first time. I know I'm not the only person to be touched deeply by the moments of that day—or by the magic of Liverpool. A couple of others who were so touched were Lennon and McCartney themselves. The city struck such a deep chord in them that, unlike many artists, they could draw on their hometown experiences while they were still there. James Joyce had to go to Paris to explore Dublin. Mark Twain wrote about the Mississippi from Hartford, Connecticut. Willa Cather wrote of the American prairie while she lived in New York City. But Lennon and McCartney drew on their Liverpool lives while they were still *living* Liverpool lives. That's how deeply felt their hometown days were.

In a sense, the John Lennon portrayed here was in his last year of adolescence. He would jump into adulthood —far too suddenly—almost exactly a year later, July 15, 1958, with his mother's death in a car accident. . . . At the time of John's own death in 1980, there was a little chest at the foot of his bed in New York City. He kept his most prized possessions there. Imprinted on the chest was a single word in capital letters: LIVERPOOL. John Lennon might not have been too sharp with the facts and dates, but he never forgot certain impressions—such as the sound of the Salvation Army Band at Strawberry Field, the smell of the leather seats on the Menlove Avenue tram, or the look of the River Mersey at midnight.

While Lennon had LIVERPOOL written on a chest, Paul McCartney has always had the word emblazoned across his heart. Like a benevolent big brother, he has frequently shown his feeling for his hometown. For example, in April of 1989, ninety-five people were tragically killed at the Football Association Cup Semifinal in Sheffield, England. Many of the dead were children and adolescents from Liverpool. To aid the disaster victims' families, McCartney participated in the rerecording of the Liverpool favorite "Ferry 'Cross the Mersey," donating his efforts.

On my plane trips home from England, I've often considered how much of life John and Paul must have seen from little turbojet windows. Their hearts must have ached to take the ferry 'cross the Mersey. Well, this book is not nearly as much fun as the ferry. But the writing was fueled by feelings as well as facts, so I hope you enjoyed this one-day ticket to ride.

ACKNOWLEDGMENTS

I would like to take a moment of your time to give my sincere thanks . . .

- to Reverend John V. Roberts, rector of St. Peter's Church, Woolton, Liverpool, for opening so many doors to people, places, and information
- to Ray Coleman, popular music's premier biographer, for encouraging me to continue corrupting the English language
- to Geoff Rhind, a classmate of John Lennon's, for the long talks and for the use of his picture of John playing at the Woolton church fête in '57
- to Rod Davis, Colin Hanton, Len Garry, and Eric Griffiths of the Quarry Men Skiffle Group for so frequently interrupting the normal course of their daily lives to answer every one of my far-too-detailed questions
- to Bob Molyneux, who made the audiotape of the

Quarry Men on the day John and Paul met, for providing me with his extensive assistance

- to Sandy Choron, my agent, for switching gears from her Boss Springsteen meetings to work so ardently with another Jersey Boy
- to David Stanford and Kristine Puopolo, my editors at Viking/Penguin, for believing in this book and leading me to improve it
- to Dan O'Toole, of the *Los Angeles Times* syndicate, for bringing my work to a larger if less sane audience
- to James C.G. Conniff of St. Peter's, for putting up with me almost every day for the better part of four years
- to Les Paul, guitar genius, for his always-ready advice and for coming through in the clutch to help my mother when she became seriously ill
- to Ivan Vaughan and the late Mary Elizabeth ("Mimi") Smith, who endured their nightmarish pains heroically, for going on the record with stories that were so integral to this story
- to Mike McCartney (Paul's brother) and Pete Shotton (John's best friend), for recalling the early days and putting their memories on paper
- to Amy Cottrell and her late husband, Harold; Pamela Rhind; Bea McKenzie; the late Gordon Knapman; Charlie Roberts; Harry and Catherine Forrest; and the late Jack Gibbons, all of Woolton, Liverpool, for sitting through particularly long interview sessions
- to Jim Rohde and Marie Lucas, of the U.S. Naval Observatory, Dept. of the Navy, for so patiently walking me through one day's sky

- to Jimmy "Juice," of the Thurmon Munson Yankee era, for making sure, during the past eight years, that I didn't just read and write, but got out to the ballgame
- to Janet Gnosspelius, of the Woolton Society, for helping "an American cousin" get the facts straight
- to my brother Mike, of the chess world, for using his computer wizardry to lighten my work load at a crucial juncture
- to Sam Leach, author of *Follow the Merseybeat Road*, for leading me to a deeper understanding of Liverpool, past and present
- to Tony Scarpa, of S.D.S., for his incredible photography, his 4 A.M. transportation through New York City streets and his general kindness
- to Phil Taylor, of the Picton Library, Liverpool, for dependable assistance, both on trans-Atlantic phone calls and in person
- to Dr. Sandra Stotsky, of Harvard University, for never letting me stop being a student
- to M.J. Wood, of the National Meteorological Archive, Berkshire, England, for quick and efficient facilitation
- and, finally, to my wife, Rosemary, with all my loving, for getting me through the difficulties of the past year. If she wasn't around, I wouldn't have been able to write this book. Actually, I wouldn't have been able to write my name.

—JIM O'DONNELL

SOURCES

The following were consulted during the researching of this book:

1. Interviews by Jim O'Donnell.
2. St. Peter's Church Garden Fête program, Saturday, July 6, 1957.
3. *Liverpool Weekly News.*
4. *South Liverpool Weekly News.*
5. 8 mm home movies, snapshots, and audio tapes of St. Peter's Church Garden Fêtes.
6. *The Liverpool and Merseyside Official Red Book for 1959.* Littlebury Bros. Ltd., 1959.
7. Pete Shotton and Nicholas Schaffner, *John Lennon: In My Life.* Stein and Day, 1983.
8. *Liverpool Echo.*
9. Michael McCartney, *Remember: The Recollections and Photographs of Michael McCartney.* Henry Holt, 1992.
10. John Lennon, *In His Own Write.* Simon and Schuster, 1964.
11. John Lennon, *A Spaniard in the Works.* Simon and Schuster, 1965.
12. Various Quarry Men recordings.
13. Picton Public Library, Liverpool, England.

14. John E. Lally and Janet B. Gnosspelius, *History of Much Woolton.* The Woolton Society, 1975.

15. Historic Newspaper Archives, Rahway, New Jersey.

16. Ivan Vaughan, *Ivan: Living With Parkinson's Disease.* Macmillan, 1986.

17. Ray Coleman, *Lennon: The Definitive Biography.* HarperPerennial, 1992.

18. "Ivan," *Horizon*, BBC 2, Dec. 3, 1984. Television program.

19. Sherwood Anderson, *Winesburg, Ohio.* Viking, 1958.

20. *Liverpool Daily Post.*

21. Mark Lewisohn, *The Beatles Live! The Ultimate Reference Book.* Henry Holt, 1986.

22. John Lennon, *Rock 'n' Roll.* Apple Records, 1975. Sound recording.

23. Woolton Public Library, Liverpool, England.

24. Michael McCartney, *Thank U Very Much: Mike McCartney's Family Album.* Granada, 1982.

25. Hugh Shimmin, *Liverpool Life: Its Pleasures, Practices and Pastimes.* Edgerton Smith and Co., 1856.

26. *Liverpool Evening Express.*

27. Julia Baird, with Geoffrey Giuliano, *John Lennon, My Brother.* Henry Holt, 1988.

28. John Lennon and Paul McCartney, "Strawberry Fields Forever," *Magical Mystery Tour.* Capitol Records, 1967. Sound recording.

29. John Lennon and Paul McCartney, "Penny Lane," *Magical Mystery Tour.* Capitol Records, 1967. Sound recording.

30. Allerton Public Library, Liverpool, England.

31. Jim Bishop, *The Day Lincoln Was Shot.* Harper and Brothers, 1955.

32. Wilfred Smith, ed., *A Scientific Survey of Merseyside.* University Press of Liverpool, 1953.

33. *The London Times.*

34. Peter Fleetwood-Hasketch, *Murray's Lancashire Architectural Guide.* John Murray, 1955.

35. Hunter Davies, *The Beatles: The Authorized Biography*, second revised edition. McGraw-Hill, 1985.

36. J. Marsh, *The Story of Woolton: Reminiscences of the Past by a Native.* Wood, Westworth and Co., 1930.

37. Pauline Lennon, *Daddy, Come Home: The True Story of John Lennon and His Father*. Angus and Robertson, 1990.

38. *The New York Times*.

39. Sam Leach, *Follow the Merseybeat Road*. Eden Publications, 1983.

40. The Woolton Society, Liverpool.

41. Quentin Hughes, *Seaport: Architecture and Townscape of Liverpool*. Lund Humphries, 1964.

42. Jann Wenner, *Lennon Remembers*. Straight Arrow, 1971.

43. Michael McCartney, *Mike Mac's White and Blacks (Plus One Color)*. Penguin, 1986.

44. George Chandler, *An Illustrated History of Liverpool*. Rondo Publications, 1972.

45. John Lennon and Paul McCartney, "In My Life," *Rubber Soul*. Capitol Records, 1965. Sound recording.

46. National Meteorological Archives, Berkshire, England.

47. Ron Freethy, *The River Mersey*. Terence Dalton Limited, 1985.

48. Terry Martin, *Liverpool Corporation Tramways, 1937–1957*. Merseyside Tramway Preservation Society, 1986.

49. *The New York Herald Tribune*.

50. George Chandler, *Liverpool*. B.T. Batsford Ltd., 1957.

51. Merseyside Maritime Museum, Liverpool, England.

52. Howard Channon, *Portrait of Liverpool*. Robert Hale and Co., 1970.

53. W. Gould and A. Hodgkiss, eds., *The Resources of Merseyside*. Liverpool University Press, 1982.

54. Herman Melville, *Redburn*. Harper, 1849.

55. John Lennon, *Menlove Avenue*. Capitol Records, 1986. Sound recording.

56. Bob Dobson, *Lancashire Nicknames and Sayings*. Dalesman, 1973.

57. Max Scheler and Astrid Kirchherr, *Liverpool Days*. Genesis Publications, 1994.

58. Stephen Peebles and Elliot Mintz, *The Lost Lennon Tapes*, radio series. Syndicated by Westwood One, 1988–1992.

59. John Lennon and Paul McCartney, "Yesterday," *Yesterday and Today*. Capitol Records, 1966. Sound recording.

60. Eric Hardy, *The Birds of the Liverpool Area*. T. Buncle and Co. Ltd., 1941.

61. National Climatic Center, Ashville, North Carolina.

62. Brian H. Tolley, *Liverpool and the American Cotton Trade*. Longman, 1978.

63. *Billboard*.

64. *Discover Beatles Liverpool: Tour Guide and Pocket Map*. Cavern City Tours.

65. Lord Moran, *Winston Churchill: The Struggle for Survival, 1940–1965*. Sphere Books, 1968.

66. Stuart Mountfield, *Western Gateway: A History of the Mersey Docks and Harbour Board*. Liverpool University Press, 1965.

67. Gerry Marsden, *Ferry 'Cross the Mersey*. Columbia Records, 1965. Sound recording.

68. Richard Whittington-Egan, *The Great Liverpool Blitz*. Gallery Press, 1987.

69. David Dimbleby and David Reynolds, *An Ocean Apart: The Relationship Between Britain and America in the Twentieth Century*. Random House, 1988.

70. J. D. Salinger, *The Catcher in the Rye*. Little, Brown and Co., 1951.

71. Philip Norman, *Shout! The Beatles in Their Generation*. Simon and Schuster, 1981.

72. Derek M. Whale, *The Liners of Liverpool II*. Countyvise, 1987.

73. William L. Langer, *An Encyclopedia of World History*. Houghton Mifflin, 1972.

74. Merseyside Museum of Labour History, Liverpool, England.

75. Richard Lawton and Catherine M. Cunningham, eds., *Merseyside: Social and Economic Studies*. Longman, 1970.

76. Martin Gilbert, *Winston S. Churchill*, vol. 8, *"Never Despair," 1945–1965*. Houghton Mifflin, 1988.

77. Carol D. Terry, *Here, There & Everywhere: The First International Beatles Bibliography, 1962–1982*. Popular Culture Ink., 1985.

78. Bill Harry, *Paperback Writers: The History of the Beatles in Print*. Avon, 1984.

79. Michael Stammers, *Sail on the Mersey*. Countyvise Limited, 1984.

80. Nathaniel Hawthorne, *Our Old Home and English Notebooks*. Houghton Mifflin, 1863.

81. J. C. Emmerson and K. Warner Radcliffe, *The Mersey at Work: Ferries*. Birkenhead Press, 1982.

82. Dept. of the Navy, U.S. Naval Observatory, Washington, D.C.

83. John R. Harris, ed., *Liverpool and Merseyside*. Kelley, 1969.

84. Deirdre Morley and Alex Laing, *Look Liverpool: Images of a Great Seaport*. Light Impressions Publications Ltd., 1985.

85. Harold Macmillan, *Riding the Storm, 1956–1959*. Macmillan, 1971.

86. Geoffrey Giuliano, *Blackbird: The Life and Times of Paul McCartney*. Dutton, 1991.

87. Lorre Crimi, *The Beatle Years*, radio series. Syndicated by Westwood One, 1992–present.

88. C. Theodore Green, ed., *The Flora of the Liverpool District*. D. Marples and Co., 1902.

89. Francois Vigier, *Change and Apathy: Liverpool and Manchester During the Industrial Revolution*. MIT Press, 1970.

90. John Lennon, *Skywriting by Word of Mouth*. Harper and Row, 1986.

91. James Joyce, *Dubliners*. Viking, 1961.

92. Piet Schreuders, Mark Lewisohn, and Adam Smith, *The Beatles London*. Hamlyn, 1994.

93. Dwight D. Eisenhower, *The White House Years: Waging Peace, 1956–1961*. Heinemann, 1966.

94. Bill Harry, *The Ultimate Beatles Encyclopedia*. Hyperion, 1992.

95. Chris Salewicz, *McCartney: The Definitive Biography*. St. Martin's Press, 1986.

96. Tom Snyder, *John Lennon: Interview with a Legend*. Karl Video Corp., 1981. Video recording.

97. Jerry Hopkins, *Elvis: A Biography*. Warner, 1972.

98. *London Evening Standard*.

99. Gerry Marsden with Ray Coleman, *I'll Never Walk Alone*. Bloomsbury, 1993.

100. John Lennon and Paul McCartney, "A Day in the Life," *Sgt. Pepper's Lonely Hearts Club Band*. Capitol Records, 1967. Sound recording.

101. Charlie Gillett, *The Sound of the City: The Rise of Rock and Roll*, revised edition. Pantheon, 1984.

102. Paul McCartney, *Paul McCartney: Composer/Artist*. Pavilion, 1981.

103. Ron Jones, *The Beatles' Liverpool*. Ron Jones, 1991.

104. David Sheff, *John Lennon and Yoko Ono: The Final Testament*. Berkley Books, 1982.

105. Herb Hendler, *Year by Year in the Rock Era*. Praeger, 1987.

106. Cynthia Lennon, *A Twist of Lennon*. Avon, 1980.

107. Richard B. Morris and Graham W. Irwin, *An Encyclopedia of the Modern World*. Harper and Row, 1970.

108. Tony Gibbs, ed., *The Coastal Navigator's Notebook*. International Marine Publishing Co., 1972.

109. Frank Unwin, *Mersey Memories*. Gallery Press, 1986.

110. The Paul McCartney World Tour Program, 1989.

111. Peter Kaye, *The Beatles in Liverpool*. Starlit Liverpool Ltd., 1987.

112. Andrew Solt and Sam Egan, *Imagine: John Lennon*. Macmillan, 1988.

113. Chuck Berry, *Chuck Berry: The Autobiography*. Harmony, 1987.

114. Dan Formento, *Rock Chronicle: A 365 Day-By-Day Journal of Significant Events in Rock History*. Delilah, 1982.

115. Kevin Gunn, Denny Somach, and Kathleen Somach, *Ticket to Ride*. Morrow, 1989.

116. Mike Evans and Ron Jones, *In the Footsteps of the Beatles*. Merseyside County Council, 1981.

117. *Rolling Stone* Magazine.

118. Eric F. Goldman, *The Crucial Decade—And After: America 1945–60*. Random House, 1960.

119. James Coleman, *The Adolescent Society*. Macmillan, 1961.

120. *Musician* Magazine.

121. *Lots of Liverpool*. Beatles Unlimited Special, 1982.

122. *Encyclopedia Britannica*, S.V. William Benton. 15th Edition.

123. Douglas Miller and Marian Nowak, *The Fifties*. Doubleday, 1977.

124. David Bacon and Norman Maslov, *The Beatles' England*. 910 Press, 1982.

125. Queensbury Group, *The Book of Key Facts*. Paddington, 1978.

126. Peter Lewis, *The 50's*. Heinemann, 1978.

127. Rolling Stone Editors, *The Ballad of John and Yoko*. Rolling Stone Press, 1982.

128. *Discover Beatles London: Tour Guide and Pocket Map*. Cavern City Tours.

129. James O'Donald Mays, *Mr. Hawthorne Goes to England: The Adventures of a Reluctant Consul*. New Forest Leaves, 1983.

130. Jeffrey Merritt, *Day by Day: The Fifties*. Facts on File, 1979.

131. The Walker Art Gallery, Liverpool, England.

132. Chris Welch, *Paul McCartney: The Definitive Biography*. Proteus, 1984.

133. Robert A. Divine, *Blowing on the Wind: The Nuclear Test Ban Debate 1954–1960*. Oxford University Press, 1978.

134. *Beatlefan* magazine.

135. Pete Fornatale, *The Story of Rock 'n' Roll*. Morrow, 1987.

136. *The Wall Street Journal.*

137. Ian Forsyth, *The Beatles' Merseyside*. S.B. Publications, 1991.

138. John Swenson, *Bill Haley*. Stein and Day, 1984.

139. *The Complete Beatles Lyrics*. Hal Leonard Publishing, 1982.

140. Linda Millgate, *The Almanac of Dates*. Harcourt, Brace, Jovanovich, 1977.

141. *The Beatles Book* magazine.

142. Bill Harry, ed., *Mersey Beat: The Beginnings of the Beatles*. Omnibus Press, 1977.

143. Andy Peebles, *The Last Lennon Tapes*. Dell, 1981.

144. Andrew Solt and David Wolper, *Imagine: John Lennon*. Warner Bros. Pictures, 1988. Film.

145. *The New York Daily News.*

146. Geoffrey Giuliano, *The Beatles: A Celebration*. Methuen, 1986.

147. Alfred Wertheimer, *Elvis '56: In the Beginning*. Collier, 1979.

148. Paul McCartney, *Give My Regards to Broad Street*. Pavilion, 1984.

149. Ray Connolly, *John Lennon, 1940–1980: A Biography*. Fontana, 1981.

150. *Billboard* Editors, *Billboard Research Aids*. Billboard Chart Research, 1981.

151. *Beatles Unlimited* magazine.

152. Chet Flippo, *Yesterday: The Unauthorized Biography of Paul McCartney*. Doubleday, 1988.

153. Derek Whale, with Eric Jackson, Neville Willasey, and Colin Hunt, *Echoes of Yesterday, Parts 1, 2 and 3. Liverpool Daily Post and Echo*, 1987.

154. Peter McCabe and Robert D. Schonfeld, *John Lennon: For the Record*. Bantam, 1984.

155. Ian Watson, *Song and Democratic Culture in Britain: An Approach to Popular Culture in Social Movements*. St. Martin's Press, 1983.

156. *Liverpool Echo* editors, *A Special Tribute to John Lennon*. Carwood Printing, 1984.

157. Robert Kingsbury, ed., *Rolling Stone Book of Days*. Straight Arrow, 1976.

158. *The Compleat Beatles*. MGM/UA Home Video, 1982. Video.

159. *Life* magazine.

160. Howard A. DeWitt, *The Beatles: Untold Tales*. Horizon, 1985.

161. John Willett, *Art and the City*. Methuen and Co. Ltd., 1967.

162. *New Musical Express*.

163. Norm N. Nite, *Rock On: The Illustrated Encyclopedia of Rock 'n' Roll*, vol. 1, *The Solid Gold Years*. Crowell, 1974.

164. Paul McCartney, *Give My Regards to Broad Street*. CBS/Fox Video, 1984. Video.

165. George Melly, *Revolt into Style*. Penguin, 1970.

166. Nicholas Schaffner, *The Beatles Forever*. Cameron House, 1977.

167. Jim Miller, ed., *The Rolling Stone Illustrated History of Rock & Roll*. Random House/Rolling Stone Press, 1980.

168. *People* magazine.

169. Ian Whitcomb, *After the Ball: Pop Music from Rag to Rock*. Penguin, 1972.

170. Ed Hanel, *The Essential Guide to Rock Books*. Omnibus, 1983.

171. *The Compleat Beatles*. Contemporary Books, 1985.

172. John Goldrosen and John Beecher, *Remembering Buddy: The Definitive Biography of Buddy Holly*. Penguin, 1987.

173. *Strawberry Fields Forever* magazine.

174. Edith Horsley, *The 1950's*. Bison Books, 1979.

175. Dick Cavett, *The Dick Cavett Show*. ABC-TV, Sept. 24, 1971.

176. Mike Evans, *The Art of the Beatles*. Beech Tree, 1984.

177. Elizabeth Thomson and David Gutman, eds., *The Lennon Companion: Twenty-Five Years of Comment*. Schirmer Books, 1988.

178. F. Scott Fitzgerald, *The Great Gatsby*. Scribner's, 1925.

179. Clive Solomon, *Record Hits: The British Top 50 Charts 1954–1976*. Omnibus, 1977.

180. *Good Day Sunshine* magazine.

181. Stephen Nugent and Charlie Gillett, eds., *Rock Almanac: Top Twenty American and British Singles and Albums of the 50s, 60s and 70s*. Doubleday, 1978.

182. Vic Garbarini, Brian Cullman, and Barbara Graustark, *Strawberry Fields Forever: John Lennon Remembered*. Delilah/Bantam, 1980.

183. Charles White, *The Life and Times of Little Richard, the Quasar of Rock*. Harmony, 1984.

184. Norman Rockwell, *My Adventures as an Illustrator*. Harry N. Abrams, Inc., 1988.

185. The Beatles Collection, City of Liverpool Public Relations Dept., 1975.

186. *Time* magazine.

187. R. Serge Denisoff and Richard A. Peterson, *The Sounds of Social Change: Studies in Popular Culture*. Rand McNally, 1972.

188. Charles Dickens, *Great Expectations*. Chapman and Hall, 1860.

189. Universal Newsreel, press conference at Pan American Airlines. Worldwide Television News Corporation, Feb. 7, 1964.

190. Phil Young and Jim Bellew, *Whitbread Book of Scouseology: An Anthology of Merseyside*. Brunswick Printing and Publishing Co., Inc.

191. George Harrison, "All Those Years Ago," *Somewhere in England*. Dark Horse Records, 1981. Sound recording.

192. *Goldmine*.

193. *World Almanac*. Newspaper Association Enterprises, 1954–1981.

194. *Across the Universe* magazine.

195. Tony Jasper, *"I Read the News Today": Great Rock and Pop Headlines*. Willow Books, 1986.

196. *The 910 Newsletter*.

197. Dave Sholin, "John Lennon: The Man, The Memory." RKO Radio, Dec. 14, 1980.

198. Peter Guralnick, *Last Train to Memphis: The Rise of Elvis Presley*. Little, Brown and Co., 1994.

199. Fenton Bresler, *The Murder of John Lennon*. Sidgwick & Jackson, 1989.

200. Paul McCartney, "Here Today," *Tug of War*. MPL/Columbia Records, 1982. Sound recording.

BIBLIOGRAPHY

Here is a wide range of Beatle books that you might enjoy.

Aldridge, Alan, ed. *The Beatles Illustrated Lyrics*. Delacorte, 1969.

————, ed. *The Beatles Illustrated Lyrics*, vol. 2. Delacorte, 1971.

Bacon, David, and Norman Maslov. *The Beatles' England*. 910 Press, 1982.

Baird, Julia, with Geoffrey Giuliano. *John Lennon, My Brother*. Henry Holt, 1988.

Baker, Glenn A. *The Beatles Down Under*. Wild and Woolley, 1982.

Bedford, Carol. *Waiting for the Beatles*. Blandford, 1984.

Benson, Harry. *The Beatles: In the Beginning*. Universe, 1993.

Best, Pete, with Patrick Doncaster. *Beatle! The Pete Best Story*. Dell, 1985.

Blake, John. *All You Needed Was Love: The Beatles after the Beatles*. Putnam/Perigee, 1981.

Braun, Michael. *Love Me Do: The Beatles' Progress*. Penguin, 1964.

Bresler, Fenton. *The Murder of John Lennon*. Sidgwick & Jackson, 1989.

Carr, Roy, and Tony Tyler. *The Beatles: An Illustrated Record*. Harmony, 1975.

Castleman, Harry, and Walter J. Podrazik. *All Together Now: The

First Complete Beatles Discography, 1961–1975. Popular Culture Ink., 1975.

Clayson, Alan. *Ringo Starr: Straight Man or Joker?* Paragon, 1992.

Coleman, Ray. *Lennon: The Definitive Biography.* HarperPerennial, 1992.

———. *The Man Who Made the Beatles: An Intimate Biography of Brian Epstein.* McGraw-Hill, 1989.

The Compleat Beatles. Contemporary Books, 1985.

The Complete Beatles Lyrics. Hal Leonard Publishing, 1982.

Connolly, Ray. *John Lennon, 1940–1980: A Biography.* Fontana, 1981.

Davies, Hunter. *The Beatles: The Authorized Biography.* Second revised edition. McGraw-Hill, 1985.

DeWitt, Howard A. *The Beatles: Untold Tales.* Horizon, 1985.

DiLello, Richard. *The Longest Cocktail Party.* Popular Culture Ink., 1983.

Epstein, Brian. *A Cellarful of Noise.* Popular Culture Ink., 1984.

Evans, Mike. *The Art of the Beatles.* Beech Tree, 1984.

———, and Ron Jones. *In the Footsteps of the Beatles.* Merseyside County Council, 1981.

Fawcett, Anthony. *John Lennon: One Day at a Time.* Grove Press, 1976.

Flippo, Chet. *Yesterday: The Unauthorized Biography of Paul McCartney.* Doubleday, 1988.

Forsyth, Ian. *The Beatles' Merseyside.* S.B. Publications, 1991.

Friede, Goldie, Robin Titone, and Sue Weiner. *The Beatles A to Z.* Eyre Methuen, 1980.

Fulpen, H. V. *The Beatles: An Illustrated Diary.* Plexus, 1982.

Gambiccini, Paul. *Paul McCartney in His Own Words.* Flash Books, 1976.

Garbarini, Vic, Brian Cullman, and Barbara Graustark. *Strawberry Fields Forever: John Lennon Remembered.* Bantam, 1980.

Giuliano, Geoffrey. *Blackbird: The Life and Times of Paul McCartney.* Dutton, 1991.

———. *Dark Horse: The Private Life of George Harrison.* Dutton, 1990.

———. *The Lost Beatles Interviews.* Dutton, 1994.

Gunn, Kevin, Denny Somach, and Kathleen Somach. *Ticket to Ride.* Morrow, 1989.

Gunther, Curt, and A.J.S. Rayl. *Beatles '64: A Hard Day's Night in America.* Doubleday, 1989.

Hamblett, Charles. *Here Are the Beatles*. Four Square Books, 1964.

Harrison, George. *I. Me. Mine*. Simon and Schuster, 1981.

Harry, Bill. *Paperback Writers: The History of the Beatles in Print*. Avon, 1984.

———. *The Ultimate Beatles Encyclopedia*. Hyperion, 1992.

———, ed. *Mersey Beat: The Beginnings of the Beatles*. Omnibus Press, 1977.

Hertsgaard, Mark. *A Day in the Life: The Music and Artistry of the Beatles*. Delacorte Press, 1995.

Hoffmann, Dezo. *With the Beatles*. Omnibus, 1982.

Hopkins, Jerry. *Yoko Ono*. Macmillan, 1986.

Howlett, Kevin. *The Beatles at the Beeb: The Story of Their Radio Career, 1962–65*. BBC, 1982.

Hutchins, Chris, and Peter Thompson. *Elvis Meets the Beatles*. Smith Gryphon, 1994.

Jones, Ron. *The Beatles' Liverpool*. Ron Jones, 1991.

Kaye, Peter. *The Beatles in Liverpool*. Starlit Liverpool Ltd., 1987.

Leach, Sam. *Follow the Merseybeat Road*. Eden Publications, 1983.

Lefcowitz, Eric, with Jim Marshall. *Tomorrow Never Knows: The Beatles' Last Concert*. Terra Firma Books, 1987.

Leigh, Spencer. *Let's Go down the Cavern*. Royal Life Insurance, 1983.

———. *Speaking Words of Wisdom: Reflections on the Beatles*. Cavern City Tours, 1991.

Lennon, Cynthia. *A Twist of Lennon*. Avon, 1980.

Lennon, John. *In His Own Write*. Simon and Schuster, 1964.

———. *Skywriting by Word of Mouth*. Harper and Row, 1986.

———. *A Spaniard in the Works*. Simon and Schuster, 1965.

Lennon, Pauline. *Daddy, Come Home: The True Story of John Lennon and His Father*. Angus and Robertson, 1990.

Lewisohn, Mark. *The Beatles Live! The Ultimate Reference Book*. Henry Holt, 1986.

———. *The Beatles Recording Sessions*. Harmony, 1988.

———. *The Complete Beatles Chronicle*. Harmony, 1992.

MacDonald, Ian. *Revolution in the Head: The Beatles' Records and the Sixties*. Henry Holt, 1994.

Marsden, Gerry, with Ray Coleman. *I'll Never Walk Alone*. Bloomsbury, 1993.

Martin, George, with Jeremy Hornsby. *All You Need Is Ears*. St. Martin's Press, 1979.

McCabe, Peter, and Robert D. Schonfeld. *Apple to the Core*. Pocket, 1972.

————. *John Lennon: For the Record*. Bantam, 1984.

McCartney, Linda. *Photographs*. MPL Communications, 1982.

McCartney, Michael. *Mike Mac's White and Blacks (Plus One Color)*. Penguin, 1986.

————. *Remember: The Recollections and Photographs of Michael McCartney*. Henry Holt, 1992.

————. *Thank U Very Much: Mike McCartney's Family Album*. Granada, 1982.

McCartney, Paul. *Give My Regards to Broad Street*. Pavilion, 1984.

————. *Paul McCartney: Composer/Artist*. Pavilion, 1981.

Michaels, Ross. *George Harrison: Yesterday and Today*. Flash Books, 1977.

Neises, Charles P., ed. *The Beatles Reader*. Popular Culture Ink., 1984.

Norman, Philip. *Shout! The Beatles in Their Generation*. Simon and Schuster, 1981.

Ono, Yoko. *John Lennon: Summer of 1980*. Perigee, 1983.

Pawlowski, Gareth L. *How They Became the Beatles: A Definitive History of the Early Years, 1960–1964*. Dutton, 1989.

Peebles, Andy. *The Last Lennon Tapes*. Dell, 1981.

Reeve, Andru J. *Turn Me On, Dead Man: The Complete Story of the Paul McCartney Death Hoax*. Popular Culture Ink., 1994.

Reinhart, Charles. *The Book of Beatles Lists*. Contemporary, 1985.

Riley, Tim. *Tell Me Why: A Beatles Commentary*. Knopf, 1988.

Rolling Stone Editors. *The Ballad of John and Yoko*. Rolling Stone Press, 1982.

Rosenbaum, Helen. *The Beatles Trivia Quiz Book*. Signet, 1978.

Salewicz, Chris. *McCartney: The Definitive Biography*. St. Martin's Press, 1986.

Schaffner, Nicholas. *The Beatles Forever*. Cameron House, 1977.

Schaumburg, Ron. *Growing Up with the Beatles*. Pyramid, 1976.

Scheler, Max, and Astrid Kirchherr. *Liverpool Days*. Genesis Publications, 1994.

Schreuders, Piet, Mark Lewisohn, and Adam Smith. *The Beatles London*. Hamlyn, 1994.

Schultheiss, Tom. *A Day in the Life: The Beatles Day-by-Day, 1960–1970.* Popular Culture Ink., 1980.

Sheff, David. *John Lennon and Yoko Ono: The Final Testament.* Berkley Books, 1982.

Shepherd, Billy. *The True Story of the Beatles.* Bantam, 1964.

Shipper, Mark. *Paperback Writer.* Grosset and Dunlap, 1978.

Shotton, Pete, and Nicholas Schaffner. *John Lennon: In My Life.* Stein and Day, 1983.

Solt, Andrew, and Sam Egan. *Imagine: John Lennon.* Macmillan, 1988.

Somach, Denny, and Ken Sharp. *Meet the Beatles . . . Again!* Musicom, 1995.

Southall, Brian. *Abbey Road.* Patrick Stephens Ltd., 1985.

Spencer, Terence. *It Was Thirty Years Ago Today.* Holt, 1994.

Stokes, Geoffrey. *The Beatles.* Rolling Stone Press/Times Books, 1981.

Sulpy, Doug, and Ray Schweighardt. *Drugs, Divorce and a Slipping Image.* The 910 Press, 1994.

Sutcliffe, Pauline, and Adam Clayson. *Backbeat: Stuart Sutcliffe: The Lost Beatle.* Pan Books, 1994.

Taylor, Alistair, with Martin Roberts. *Yesterday: The Beatles Remembered.* Sidgwick & Jackson, 1988.

Taylor, Derek. *As Time Goes By: Living in the Sixties.* Straight Arrow, 1973.

———. *It Was Twenty Years Ago Today.* Simon and Schuster, 1987.

Terry, Carol D. *Here, There & Everywhere: The First International Beatles Bibliography, 1962–1982.* Popular Culture Ink., 1985.

Thomson, Elizabeth, and David Gutman, eds. *The Lennon Companion: Twenty-Five Years of Comment.* Schirmer Books, 1988.

Turner, Steve. *A Hard Day's Write: The Stories Behind Every Beatles' Song.* HarperPerennial, 1994.

Welch, Chris. *Paul McCartney: The Definitive Biography.* Proteus, 1984.

Wenner, Jann. *Lennon Remembers.* Straight Arrow, 1971.

Wiener, Allen J. *The Beatles: The Ultimate Recording Guide.* Bob Adams, Inc., 1994.

Wiener, Jon. *Come Together: John Lennon in His Time.* Random House, 1984.

Williams, Allan, and William Marshall. *The Man Who Gave the Beatles Away.* Macmillan, 1975.

Woffinden, Bob. *The Beatles Apart.* Proteus, 1981.

INDEX

FOR THE BEST IN PAPERBACKS, LOOK FOR THE

In every corner of the world, on every subject under the sun, Penguin represents quality and variety—the very best in publishing today.

For complete information about books available from Penguin—including Puffins, Penguin Classics, and Arkana—and how to order them, write to us at the appropriate address below. Please note that for copyright reasons the selection of books varies from country to country.

In the United Kingdom: Please write to *Dept. JC, Penguin Books Ltd, FREEPOST, West Drayton, Middlesex UB7 0BR*.

If you have any difficulty in obtaining a title, please send your order with the correct money, plus ten percent for postage and packaging, to *P.O. Box No. 11, West Drayton, Middlesex UB7 0BR*

In the United States: Please write to *Consumer Sales, Penguin USA, P.O. Box 999, Dept. 17109, Bergenfield, New Jersey 07621-0120*. VISA and MasterCard holders call 1-800-253-6476 to order all Penguin titles

In Canada: Please write to *Penguin Books Canada Ltd, 10 Alcorn Avenue, Suite 300, Toronto, Ontario M4V 3B2*

In Australia: Please write to *Penguin Books Australia Ltd, P.O. Box 257, Ringwood, Victoria 3134*

In New Zealand: Please write to *Penguin Books (NZ) Ltd, Private Bag 102902, North Shore Mail Centre, Auckland 10*

In India: Please write to *Penguin Books India Pvt Ltd, 706 Eros Apartments, 56 Nehru Place, New Delhi 110 019*

In the Netherlands: Please write to *Penguin Books Netherlands bv, Postbus 3507, NL-1001 AH Amsterdam*

In Germany: Please write to *Penguin Books Deutschland GmbH, Metzlerstrasse 26, 60594 Frankfurt am Main*

In Spain: Please write to *Penguin Books S. A., Bravo Murillo 19, 1° B, 28015 Madrid*

In Italy: Please write to *Penguin Italia s.r.l., Via Felice Casati 20, I-20124 Milano*

In France: Please write to *Penguin France S. A., 17 rue Lejeune, F–31000 Toulouse*

In Japan: Please write to *Penguin Books Japan, Ishikiribashi Building, 2–5–4, Suido, Bunkyo-ku, Tokyo 112*

In Greece: Please write to *Penguin Hellas Ltd, Dimocritou 3, GR–106 71 Athens*

In South Africa: Please write to *Longman Penguin Southern Africa (Pty) Ltd, Private Bag X08, Bertsham 2013*